THREE-FINGER ZEN

THREE-FINGER ZEN

A BASKETBALL REVOLUTION

XIAOXING (BENJAMIN) CHEN

iUniverse, Inc.
Bloomington

THREE-FINGER ZEN
A Basketball Revolution

iUniverse books may be ordered through booksellers or by contacting:

iUniverse
1663 Liberty Drive
Bloomington, IN 47403
www.iuniverse.com
1-800-Authors (1-800-288-4677)

ISBN: 978-1-4620-4717-8 (sc)
ISBN: 978-1-4620-4718-5 (ebk)

Printed in the United States of America

iUniverse rev. date: 08/23/2011

To God, thank You for helping me to find my way.
To my parents, my wife Xuming, thank you for your love and support of my endeavors.

CONTENTS

Introduction

Over the past century, basketball has evolved from a simple indoor physical exercise to a game of team competition and indoor/outdoor recreation and a professional sport worldwide. As a sport, basketball gives its participants an overall workout by involving most upper and lower bodies in basic human physical activities: running, jumping, and throwing. As a game, it is attractive, in its fascinate team offense/defense executions with excellent individual skills and athletic performances, for most people to watch, to participate, or to compete. Nevertheless, modern basketball faces major challenges and obstacles for further development, caused directly by its own technical problems and limitations.

Technical Problems

Making baskets for higher scores is the sole objective of a competition basketball game. The existing scoring methods include regular shots, layups, hook shots, and other shooting throws. In the past five decades, the two-hand over-the-head shooting technique has been commonly applied in competition games of different levels (professional, college, and youth games) as a standard or **conventional shooting method.**

The conventional method takes a shooting form of *straight body posture* and *elbow-in/index-finger-release alignment* on *two-footed jumping* push. It has advantages in triple threat (pass/dribble/shoot) shot set, and high, flexible release. However, this method lacks shooting dynamics and compatibilities with many key elements of the sport.

- ✘ It's irrelevant to players' major athletic abilities of running, throwing, turning, and one-footed jumping.
- ✘ It can not be applied to other scoring methods, such as layups and hook shots.
- ✘ It's incompatible to the fundamental ball-handling skills of dribbling and passing.

Technically, the conventional shooting method has the following vital problems:

- ✘ **An isolated shooting process.** The conventional shooting mechanics, composed of the techniques of *squared feet*, *elbow-in alignment*, *over-the-head set*, *two-hand push*, and *index-finger release*, are designed and used only for shooting the basketball. It is nearly impossible to adapt the shooting techniques to dribble, to do layups or hooks, or even to pass the ball.

✘ **Limited shooting power and control.** In the shooting process, limited muscle groups and body movements are involved in its short shooting push, about the distance of a forearm extension; therefore, limited shooting power is generated. From shot set to release, as a conventional technique, the first three fingers—thumb and index and middle fingers—primarily control the ball. On shooting release, it is difficult to use these three fingers to control the ball's flying directions, arcs, and spins.

✘ **Short ranges and low accuracies.** Lacking power and control, the method produces poor shooting range and accuracy. It is evident that professional basketball games yield average shooting percentages of less than 50 percent in the NBA, with about 30 percent in the three-point ranges. With the conventional shooting techniques, most players cannot generate enough shooting power and accurately control the ball in the shooting process.

✘ **Vulnerable to defensive interferences.** There is no protective mechanism in the shooting process. The ball is exposed to the defense during the whole process. Therefore, it is extremely vulnerable to defensive attacks, such as steal, slap, block, or hand-in-face interference.

✘ **Uniform shooting posture.** Square-up over-the-head shooting is the only body form of the method. It makes the shooting predictable, thus vulnerable to help defense. The straight shooting form and mechanical shooting rhythms, with multiple stops (catch, set, and shot pauses), allow defense the time to react and reach.

✘ **The shooting mechanics don't work for every player.** In the NBA, only a few shooters can accurately master the rigid shooting mechanics with good shooting alignment and posture. Naturally, most players cannot handle elbow-in alignment and index-finger-release techniques. They have to shoot this way all the time, even with low shooting percentages, because there is no other shooting technique available.

✘ **Some players can't shoot at all.** A number of key professional players cannot make field goals with the shooting method, so they just hook, layup, or dunk. Because of having bad shooting mechanics, they are poor free throwers, with a shooting percentage of around 60 percent as compared to the average of about 80 percent of other players (www.nba.com).

The Values and Challenges of the Game

There is no doubt that basketball is an asset to human society.

As a game, basketball is attractive in its sporting nature of getting people involved. There is no age limit or physical requirement to play the game, as long as you can pick up the ball and throw it into basket. The playing conditions are simple: all you need is a ball, a basket, and a little court. It has become evermore popular among the general public because it's a fun workout as well as an enjoyable spectator's game.

Playing or practicing basketball promotes the physical and mental health of participants. Compared to soccer, the most popular sport in the world, basketball engages substantially more active upper body activities of its players. Besides competitions with prime participation of young athletic players, working out in basketball games has great value in physical conditioning, mental acuity training, and interpersonal contact for all age groups.

In elementary and secondary schools, basketball is an integral part of physical education. A great team and individual sport, it facilitates physical and mental development in children. By playing basketball in and out of school, they can learn about teamwork, make friends, and get good physical exercise.

Nevertheless, basketball is not without problems.

During the past few decades, basketball has developed into a professional game and a popular sport worldwide. High-level professional competitions promote the game and attract more young people to seriously train for the sport. This cohesive development brings mixed effects and influences to our society, especially with younger generations.

✘ **Products.** Nowadays there are many vocations in the sport besides players, coaches, and sports teachers. Professional teams have offense/defense coordinators, shooting/free throw coaches, individual coaches/trainers, strength/conditioning trainers, nutrition/rehab specialists, and other basketball-related professionals. The assisting staff members help players improve their performance but lower their working intelligence. Because everything is tightly regulated for the game, all they have to do is to follow instructions.

✘ **By-products.** Professionalism produces many by-products: basketball idols, commercialization, overpriced sporting goods, and undereducated players.

✘ **Undereducated players.** Professional players project heavy influences on young basketball players. Most talented school athletes share the same dream of becoming a basketball star with multimillion-dollar contracts, lucrative sponsorships, and publicity. Many of them try to push for a basketball career in the early ages, leaving their education behind.

✘ **Public images.** Professional basketball players have mixed public images. It is commonly acceptable to the general public that they lack literacy and basic knowledge due to subpar education. Fancy lifestyles, gambling, sex scandals, and domestic violence have been exposed in their private lives. The majority of NBA players declared bankruptcy just five years after retiring, for their lack of education negatively affected their asset management abilities (*Sports Illustrated*, March 23, 2009).

✘ **Bad basketball.** Professional basketball emphasizes individual talents and physical powers. Driven by the individualism and selfishness, many young players take the game as exhibition of their basketball talents and physical strengths. Consequently, it brings to the game many ugly plays and misconduct, such as aggressive body contact, low-post wresting, one-man team, dangerous fouls, disrespectful language and gestures, and even fights. This type of game misleads the public, especially youths, as to the way of playing basketball, hindering healthy development of the sport.

✘ **Physical games.** Influenced by professional games, the power-over-skill concept builds up among young players. This is the reason that there are so many overweight amateur basketball players. They enjoy playing with body weight and strength in the lower posts, prefer explosive power to endurance and agility, and have more upper body strength than lower body athletics.

✘ **Unsuccessful careers.** Many high school and college players could not make professional leagues. As they gambled for basketball careers when young, their educations were left behind for the rest of their lives. Even with the most elite college players selected by professional leagues, their limited educations won't cope with the complexity of high-level competition and training. All they can do is to follow the instructions of their coaches and trainers. Even when they are injured, they have to persist in their training for demanding games. That would expose them to higher reinjuring risks, and some might be career ending.

The Way to Perfection

Can basketball be a perfect game?

Yes, basketball can be a perfect game. It should be a beautiful game that everyone loves playing and enjoys watching. It should be a great sport that enhances physical and mental development in youths. Playing basketball should add value to our daily lives, with overall body workouts and promoted public health. It should be an exciting, civilized game that encourages healthy physical contact and avoids any physical meanness. The basketball court should be a place of vivid physical activity, filled with friendly contests, enjoyment, and teamwork, not a place of disrespectfulness, physical discrimination, or any kind of misconduct. Basketball can be a perfect game for participants of all ages and genders, and that would add pure value to the human societies.

A New Way of Playing Basketball

The history of basketball is the evolution of different ball skills and playing styles. In the last three decades, however, the game has developed to a high-level competition with little technical improvement. Modern basketball has met a bottleneck in the game's advancement.

The discovery of *3fz*, **Three-Finger Zen,** *breaks* the norm and leads the way to basketball perfection. Three-Finger Zen, technically called **Universal Ball-Handling Mechanism**, is a natural, innate mechanism in the human hand and arm for artisan works and sports. Distinctive from the conventional ball skills, *3fz* applies primarily *the last three fingers—**MAP:** middle finger, annular (ring) finger, and pinky—to handle and control the ball, and the **ring finger** has a command-and-control role in the ball-handling processes of dribbling, passing, and shooting.

The *3fz* mechanism is an integration of individual ball-handling skills, and it leads a new way of playing basketball offense and defense. It is easy to learn, compared to any of the conventional skills, and is suitable for everyone. In a short two to three years of systematic *3fz* training, you can become one of the best basketball players in the leagues you are playing, no matter how small or weak you are, as long as you have good health and learning abilities. In other words, by mastering *3fz*, an average amateur basketball player will eventually be able to beat (one-on-one) the best players in the world.

The Discovery of Three-Finger Zen

In 2009, after five years of basketball practice and praying to God, I found Three-Finger Zen, a Universal Ball-Handling Mechanism of our arms and hands. A unique basketball-handling skill, it gives us precise ball control and produces superiorly accurate shooting. Without the constraints of the conventional skills and techniques, I entered an unknown domain and found the treasure, a pure, natural mechanism of one's body that leads to basketball excellence, which has been ignored by the basketball world. The three major factors of my *3fz* discovery are my **unconventional playing style**, **educational background**, and **belief in God's work**.

Unconventional Playing Style

I grew up as a teenager in a military academy in Beijing in the late 1960s. For an extended period, we had no school because of the notorious Cultural Revolution in China. The only outdoor joy I can remember from that time was watching people playing basketball. My curiosity was intense, and I soon had two important findings: First, there is no boring basketball game, no matter how poorly players are playing, because every move is unique. Second, every play of basketball can be performed differently and more creatively. Today I realize that these findings are so true as far as modern basketball games.

In middle school, I always wanted to go to the basketball courts. I couldn't get many chances to play, since there might be twenty students chasing one ball. But nothing could stop my imagination, and I always fantasized myself handling a basketball with fancy plays full of creativity. For me, basketball is not just a wonderful game; it's a dream as well.

Throughout college, I never received any coaching, and that persistently allowed me to play basketball in the style I imagined. I deemed basketball a game of pure skills and creative movements. With such perception, I could occasionally play some good games; however, I had never been good when facing physical challenges.

In 1992, I came to the United States for graduate study in environmental health sciences at UCLA. In my leisure time, I read John R. Wooden's *Pyramid of Success and Leadership* and his other works, and watched college and professional basketball games. It struck me that basketball is not only a sport but also a science, an art, and a philosophy of life. Coach Wooden taught every single aspect of basketball.

Then I began to study and play basketball seriously in competitive games. Amazingly, I realized that my knowledge in engineering, biology, and health sciences was applicable to basketball games. Basketball is not just a physical workout; its game concepts and training need profound understanding in the sport's theories and principles and physical conditioning to guide practice. In praxis with educated new approaches, I improved my basketball skills and games dramatically. Now a senior player, I still play competitive games with the sport's fundamentals and creativity.

For a long time, I tried to use full resources of my body and mind in my basketball training and games by applying all five fingers to control the ball. Eventually, I found out that the last three fingers

(*MAP*) are more dynamic and powerful in controlling the basketball than the first three, and this led to my *3fz* discovery.

A Perfect Game

The basketball game I dream about is a perfect game, a competition of pure skills and excellent athletics, a sport of smart physical contact and team spirit, a platform where great personal virtues and physical beauties are exhibited, and a friendly game that everybody loves to play.

My dream is shared with Pierre de Coubertin, a founder of the modern Olympics, in his *Ode au Sport*: "A sport as the delights of Gods, distillation of lift; it is beauty, just, daring, honor, joy, fecundity, progress and peace." We basketball advocators can change it to the game it should be:

- **A wonderful sport** exploring maximum human physical abilities and athletic talents
- **A competition of pure skills and athletic excellence**, and participated in by all, regardless of age, gender, or size
- **A spectacular game** full of accurate dynamic shots, athletic moves, and fluent team plays; exciting to play and watch
- **A beautiful game** of sportsmanship and physical esthetics
- **A healthy sport** improving physical and mental development in children and the public, as well as in relationships
- **A clean game** that is played fairly and justly, filled with individual and group virtues, and free of dirty plays, malicious physical contact, or any misconduct
- **A sport protecting players from passive injuries** so that they will have long sports lives
- **A friendly game** to win hearts and bring love and peace

What We Shall Do

So how to perfect the game of basketball? A perfect basketball game seems to be a good concept or an imaginary goal, unrealistic to achieve, rather than a practical objective.

Not to worry! Let it be, and let it go with the nature. "Man follows the earth, the earth the universe, the universe the Tao (the Way), and the Tao follows the Nature." Laozi (Lao-Tzu) told us *what to do* 2,500 years ago in *Dao De Jing* (*Tao Te Ching*).

"God created man in His image . . . male and female He created them" (Gen. 1:27). Sports are re-creations of the created, for its spirits come from the Holy Spirit, and ways of doing are led by the Way. In His image, we are blessed to enjoy our physical talents in sports, not just to labor our bodies for survival; we exhilarate ourselves by winning spirits in fair competitions, rather than in brutal fights and wars. The Bible also teaches us *how to do* in every aspect of our lives and sports.

Basketball has evolved naturally, with simple purposes of team working and physical exercises, to a creative sport. Over one hundred years, the popular sport has developed into a high-level competition game. However, the essences of basketball never change.

To make the dream become reality, we still need a push. Now we have a tool, a natural talent given to us for handling the basketball. It is an innate mechanism that human beings used for thousand of years in their daily living, artistic works, and sporting activities. This mechanism is *3fz*—Three-Finger Zen—Universal Ball-Handling Mechanism.

A Master's Teaching

Five century ago, Leonardo da Vinci revealed the secrets of human creativity as a body cross in his famous painting *Vitruvian Man*. Vertically, man is created in the image of God, with the brain of infinite resource and the body of abundant love. Horizontally, with the outstretched hands, human can touch, handle, and re-create the outside worlds by doing. Internally, from the left hand and arm across the body to the right arm and hand, and vice versa, there is the way of doing and interacting with the world, guided by the Holy Spirit of the symbolic Holy Cross.

In *Vitruvian Man*, Leonardo clearly depicted the functions of human fingers: index finger to tell, thumb to support, middle finger to reach, and ring and little fingers to touch and move (natural pronation, palming down, of the uplifted hands). The last three fingers, *MAP*, are outstretched, with the straight ring fingers as the horizontal axis of the Cross. In the uplifted hand, the thumb points precisely to the radial tip of the ring finger, telling us that the two fingers are uniquely aligned. It is the *MAP* that leads to treasures of our holy (not dirty) bodies, of abundant resources and love in our brains and hands.

Thankfully I find it, **the Tao**—"the Way"—of playing basketball. In this book, I will share with you every secret of the way to basketball excellence. It is for everyone, no matter if you are short, weak, or old. The Tao leads to a meaningful life in basketball.

SUMMARY OF 3fz TECHNIQUES

3fz

Full Name:	**Three-Finger Zen**
Technical Name:	**Universal Ball-Handling Mechanism**
Meanings:	*Three Fingers (**MAP**)*: Middle finger, Annular (ring) finger, and Pinky (little finger) *Zen*: the way of understanding and manipulating basketball
Description:	A one-hand ball-handling skill by actively controlling the ball with the three fingertips, while thumb and index fingers are passively involved to support the ball
	In a ball-handling process (dribble, pass, or shoot), it comprises *MAP* catch, Finger-Spring Cup (*FSC*) control, and *MAP* release of the basketball.
	In ball-handling processes, Universal Alignment (*4u1*) of hand is maintained for precise ball control.

UniShot

Technical Name:	**Universal Shooting Mechanism**
Description:	*3fz* application in shooting the basketball with the non-shooting hand's assistance
	Reverse-Finger Twist (RFT) is a key technique added to *3fz* for setting a *UniShot*.

Low-Hand *UniShot*: An underhanded shot, it takes the form of a regular layup by shooting the ball with hand supination—palming up.

Up-Hand *UniShot*: It takes a mixed form of the conventional shooting in hand and arm posture and hook shots' high release positions by shooting the ball with hand pronation—palming down.

4u1

Technical Name: **Universal Alignment**

Description: The neural connections and biomechanical associations (via palm) in the hand between the first (thumb) and fourth (ring) fingers, in a form of fully opposed thumb and abducted fingers of an open hand, to transfer power and control to the basketball in ball-handling processes

A precise relative positioning of five fingers on the surface of basketball, adjustable through ball manipulations of thumb and ring finger for different ball handlings

A geometric curve of the hand, along the inner sideline (to middle finger) of the ring finger to the thumb tip, focusing the center of basketball and aligning the ball to a target

An adjustable tip-to-tip alignment, by twisting fingers with a pivot at the ring finger, for shooting, passing, or dribbling basketball

Shooting *4u1*: Inner tips alignment of thumb and ring finger for up-hand *UniShot*

Passing *4u1*: Alignment of the inner tip of ring finger to the middle tip of thumb for passing or low-hand *UniShot*

Dribbling *4u1*: The outer tip of thumb and the inner/middle tip of ring finger alignment for dribbling

FSC

Full Name: **Finger-Spring Cup**

Description: A *3fz* component

A flexible, imaginary cup of the hand formed with five fingertips as brim, dynamically sucking or holding the ball in changing directions dictated by *4u1*

Variable in sizes by adducting/abducting the thumb

RFT

Full Name: **Reverse-Finger Twist**

Description: A *UniShot* component

A shot-setting technique with two hands holding and twisting the ball on its opposite sides in reversed directions

Chapter 1

Basketball Revolution

WHY A REVOLUTION?

Basketball is a wonderful game, exciting to play and enjoyable to watch. It has tremendous popularity worldwide, being the second most participated sport after soccer. There are established administration and competition systems of all levels: the International Basketball Federation (FIBA), national and local basketball organizations, professional basketball leagues such as the NBA and Euroleague, college leagues like the NCAA, and youth leagues.

Throughout the world, basketball players, coaches, trainers, and teachers dedicate themselves to the sport. We have sports institutions, researchers, and practitioners who focus their works on basketball studies and training. Basketball facilities are sophisticated and well built in many countries; some of them are magnificent landmarks of their cities.

Basketball seems to be a great sport with perfect systems. What is wrong with basketball, and why do we need a revolution?

We do have wonderful basketball games and nearly perfect systems. But to become a perfect game and a pure, healthy sport, it has still a long way to go. For the future game we dream of, the modern basketball, with its technical limitations, can do little by itself. In contrary, the existing basketball techniques negatively affect the development of basketball in many ways, as we will discuss in the following sections of this chapter. Therefore, a revolution is necessary for a new, advanced game of basketball.

This revolution is not about organizational or structural changes like the Marxist revolution; we want our good games and systems intact. It is a pure technological revolution of fundamental basketball techniques and skills. Similarly, in the Industrial Revolution and the information revolution, machines and computers replaced hard laborers and those doing paperwork. Now, for basketball, *3fz* will replace the existing ball-handling techniques and offense skills, all of them. In other words, today's basketball offense skills, especially shooting skills, will be obsolete in the revolution.

In contrast to the industrial and information revolutions, which have been both good and bad, the *3fz* revolution will bring only positive changes to basketball. It will significantly improve every aspect of the game, solve the existing problems, and benefit every participant of the sport.

For the basketball revolution, we have established theories, mechanisms and techniques, and successful praxes. Human kinetics and hand studies are the scientific foundations of the revolution. **Universal Ball-Handling Mechanism** (*3fz*), **Universal Shooting Mechanism** (*UniShot*), and **Universal Alignment** (*4u1*) are the new groundbreaking mechanisms and techniques. These revolutionary skills are acquired in my long-term praxis, and they have been successfully experimented and tested among youths.

Prior to the engagement of the big changes, we ought to know, from a revolutionary perspective, what problems and challenges are obstacles in the advancement of basketball.

CURRENT SITUATIONS AND CHALLENGES

Modern basketball favors big, strong, and quick players. It is disadvantageous to small, female, and older players for their lack of size, strength, agility, or explosive power. A competitive basketball game is full of intensive physical activity and bodily contact. Players of competitive basketball leagues are well conditioned for tough physical challenges. They need to have excellent athletic strengths to apply their ball skills in competitions.

Having distinctive athletic bodies, females play a different style of basketball than males play. There are great women's games, with fluent teamwork, spectacular passes, swift transitions, and accurate shots. But physical basketball games are extremely hazardous to most female players. Due to their special physiques, women endure higher risks of injury during extreme movements or activities. For instance, during a hard stop or sudden direction change, compared to their male counterparts, female players are exposed to significantly higher risk of a torn ACL—anterior cruciate ligament—a crucial ligament of the knee joint involved in jumping and turning.

Basketball is among the sports leading in injuries, and injury is the main cause of short careers of many professional players. Without any protective equipment, players collide, hit and foul each other, or fall and land improperly after jumping, and they get hurt. The higher the level of competition, the more risks of injury professional players are exposed to.

Modern basketball has two major challenges: *technical limitation* and *playing style*. In the last thirty years of basketball development, there has been no significant technical improvement or innovative skill of any kind, but the players are younger and stronger, with more physical powers. More teenagers have entered professional basketball leagues, and there are significant increases in the three-point distances—about two feet (half a meter)—in the NBA and FIBA games.

The technical limitations of the conventional basketball lead to physical playing styles, as pumping muscles for brutal strengths in offense and pressing with rough body contacts in defense are easy ways to elevate the game for public attractions. Consequently, modern basketball games develop to a "physical powers over pure skills" playing style. Professional players may be more skilled than amateurs, but their physical powers are definitely superior. Unfortunately, there are more bad (or ugly) basketball games coming along with the playing style.

Isolated Offensive Skills

The individual basketball skills, including pass, dribble, and shoot, are fundamental components of team offense. Each of them uses different ball-handling techniques. They are independent offensive skills and thus trained separately.

On the other hand, players have variable talents in mastering the skills. Point guards are normally good at dribbling and passing but not necessarily at shooting. Many professional players cannot pass the ball with good control, especially in dynamic game settings, so they rarely have assists in their games. Shoot on catch is a skill that only a few great shooters have mastered.

While training, players must allocate extra time to practice each of the isolated skills. Even in the same skill category, like passing, different types of passes are practiced in distinctive drills. For scoring, jump shots, hook shots, and layups are using totally different techniques. Regardless of a player's talent level, separated time and effort are needed to acquire each type of the categorized skills.

Pass and Catch

Passing is the most difficult ball-handling skill. Timing, vision, experience, and technique are important elements of a good pass in dynamic game settings. Players' talents and hard training are needed to integrate the elements and throw assisting passes in the game. In the top professional leagues such as the NBA, only a handful of players can make accurate assisting passes facing defensive pressure. For passing, there are no standard techniques and no definite body posture, hand-arm involvement, or footwork. Passing skills are irrelevant to dribbling and shooting skills.

From ball release positions, there are three types of passing skills, each with specific techniques:

- **Chest pass.** Ball is held to the middle front section of body. It is a two-handed symmetric pass powered primarily by the chest and legs. The pass is quick, safe, and good with triple threat combination, but it is hard to throw long passes such as crosscourt passes.

- **Lob pass.** Ball is to a side of body. A lob pass is a complex of ball catch and quick throw. The pass has usually a one-handed release with a combined hand-arm action. It requires excellent coordination of arms and legs, court vision, decision making, and teamwork.

- **Over-the-head pass.** Two-handed or one-handed over-the-head passes have no definite forms. Players just throw overhead passes with their own styles, feelings, and abilities.

The major challenge is that there is no set passing alignment of arm, hand, and fingers on ball. That makes it difficult to coordinate shoulder, elbow, wrist, and fingertips to catch and throw the ball with good control. Mechanically, holding a big basketball without precise finger alignment, even with the good aerodynamics of a round ball in smaller distances, makes it difficult to throw accurate long passes like the passes in American football.

Catching the ball seems not as hard as passing it. But if you try to catch the ball with one hand in the air with control, simultaneously keep body balance, and get ready to pass or shoot, it is not easy at all. There is no set mechanism for catching the ball; technically, it is just a wild catch every time a player receives a pass.

Dribble

Dribbling is the most misused skill in basketball offense. Nowadays, professional players tend to be more confident in their dribbling skills, as they are allowed to change the ball directions twice in one dribble without it being called palming. Selfishness or heroism is another factor for overconfident one-man shows. Most players have developed a bad dribble-first habit, which gives the defense time to kill their offensive chances effectively.

Conventional dribbling emphasizes active hand and arm involvements in handling the basketball, but there is no standard finger alignment controlling the ball. That is the reason that players are dribbling the ball in quite different forms and postures, even for a simple crossover. Actually, players are using different nonstandard techniques for each of the following three types of dribbling:

- **Ball on side:** Inside-out, back-and-forth, and speed dribbles
- **Ball in front:** Crossover and cross-the-legs dribbles
- **Ball at rear:** Behind-the-back, spin-move, and back cross-the-legs dribbles.

The three dribbling types have distinctive ball-controlling techniques, which are not transferrable and must be trained separately. Therefore, many players can't dribble a crossover, and some don't do behind-the-back or spin-move dribbles. Because there is no technical standard to follow, many players just couldn't figure out the physical coordination of some dribbling types in their skill development.

More detailed technical analyses of passing techniques and Universal Ball-Handling Mechanism are given in chapter 2.

Shoot

Shooting is the most important, complex, and therefore the most trained skill of basketball offense. The existing two-hand over-the-head method has been taught by coaches and teachers as a standard shooting technique for making field goals. Despite its practical use in games and worldwide acceptance by basketball players and coaches, the conventional shooting method has vital defects: *shooting alignment* and *posture*.

From defensive perspectives, the conventional shooting is uniform, predictable, and unprotected. It is evident that players' shooting percentages decline dramatically in the games (about 50 percent drop in the NBA), as compared to their shooting practices. No doubt defense presence is the difference maker. In other words, the shooting is extremely vulnerable to defense. With that in mind, coaches have a straight goal of creating open shots in training their team offense.

The conventional shooting alignment is based on elbow-in and index-finger-release mechanics. Biomechanically, this alignment is contradictory to human physiology and kinesiology. (Please read chapter 4 for the analysis on the shooting alignment and the detailed technical analyses of shooting problems.) In the shooting mechanics and their compact processes, it is hard for players to control the ball or to generate enough shooting power for long shots.

These vital problems can't be solved by the conventional shooting method itself since the defects lie in the shooting mechanics. A change for new shooting techniques is needed.

Ugly Basketball Games

From its invention to modern games, basketball exhibits its unique, attractive essence with three important attributes:

- **A healthy sport.** The sport gives its participants a good overall workout, improves physical strength and mental acuity, and promotes good general health.
- **A civilized game.** As a game of pure competition in skills and athletics, it exhibits great team spirit and personal virtue, bringing friendship and love among participants and teams.
- **An enjoyable game.** It is a game full of spectacular drives and shots, powerful moves, graceful layups, dreamlike passes, tacit team plays, and so forth. It is one of the most enjoyable and exciting sports to play and to watch.

But in certain stages of development, with **technical limitations** of modern basketball and **negative influence** of professionalism, basketball competitions oftentimes turn out to be quite ugly. The followings are the negative sides of the game:

- ✗ **Physical Games.** When a game gets physical, it is tough to play or even to watch. Rough physical contact stimulates the wartime fighting spirits of human nature, causing total ignorance of the sport's essences. Emotional talks, dangerous offensive or defensive maneuvers, hard or flagrant fouls, and fights or brawls are common symptoms of a physical game. They severely damage the game. A fighting game exposes players to extreme professional hazards: frustration, emotional outbreak, and physical injuries. It brings negative public images; some were nightmares of basketball lovers.

- ✗ **Women Play in Men's Style.** Women's basketball is enjoyable for their special playing styles. Nowadays in certain professional leagues, female players try to play the game like their male counterparts. Without the jump abilities and explosive powers, it is not quite feasible for them to play that way. Shooting long jumpers, throwing crosscourt passes, and dunking the ball are not to their advantages. Some women's professional basketball games are less enjoyable, especially when they hassle each other by hand checking or scrambling for loose balls.

- ✗ **Strength over Skill.** Professional basketball hails individual talent and physical power. Low-post power moves, one-man team, and tough-pressing defense become major winning strategies of many teams. Players have to train harder for pure physical strength, which greatly compromises their athletic bodies by gaining muscle mass and body weight. Smart skills are compensated by hard muscles and brutal strength.

✘ **Overweight Amateur Players.** Obesity is a major public health issue that well presents in amateur players. Quite a proportion of players enjoy playing basketball by taking advantage of their heavier bodies. Influenced by professionals, instead of having muscle strengths, they try to beat the defense in low-posts by using their obese bodies. They move more laterally or back-down than run and jump, and they hardly have any endurance or agility in full-court games. Basketball is not healthy for them in the playing style, and it is also hazardous to play defense against them.

✘ **Ugly Physiques.** Under physical pressure because of competitive games, professionals have to train extremely hard for pure muscle strength. Instead of achieving more athletic ability, such as endurance and agility, they tend to abuse their bodies in the gym to gain fast-growing bulk muscles for short-term sport-specific advantages. Many players have bigger upper bodies and leaner lower bodies, and some are so muscular or corpulent that it affects their athletic skills.

Following the professional trends, it is more convenient for basketball players to gain physical strength than hard-trained skills. Compared with the populations of other sports, such as soccer, tennis, track and field, and swimming, basketball players have unnatural physical appearances. With their natural fitness, female track athletes and tennis players are more attractive. In contrast, female disc throwers and basketball players have more muscles but less natural beauty.

✘ **Hand-in-Face Defense.** The conventional jump shot yields low basket production for its vulnerabilities to defensive interferences. No matter how you get yourself open to shoot the ball, the least your defender can always do is to put a hand to your face. It is usually just an intimidation of the defense, for there is no chance to block the shot or even the shooter's vision.

Professional players are subtle in their tactics of hand-in-face defense. Some swing hands close to shooters' faces, like a slap, and others stick hands close to shooters' eyes as if to poke them. There have been incidents of poked eyes, bleeding noses, and slapped faces of hand-in-face defense in professional games.

Whether it is malicious or not, hand-in-face defense is an ugly act for the following reasons, and it should not be a part of the game.

* It is not sportsmanlike conduct. Rather than showing defensive skills, you just irk the shooter with a malicious gesture.
* Intentionally pointing fingers close to someone's eyes is a dangerous act.
* Hand-in-face tactics are ugly to the spectators, even if there is no contact. It is a negative part of the game.
* It is not a skill young people should learn; it is only good for defensive slackers.

When there is no chance of challenging the shot, hand-in-face defensive should be called a foul for pure intimidation. It should be eliminated permanently from the game with innovative technical solutions.

✘ Hard Fouls. In competitive or close games, one-on-one layups are the most vulnerable or dangerous of hard fouls. "No easy basket!" is a defense slogan of any team. If you jump high and try to overpower your opponent, you are highly exposed to hard fouls. You can beat defense with speed or jump, but you can't beat the pushing hands or malicious fouls. Injuries, fights, and ejections are usual consequences of these deteriorated situations.

✘ Dirty Plays. Basketball is a compact game, considering ten big players are jammed in a small area mainly covered by the three-point arc. It is difficult for referees to watch every little act of ten players, which could be well-practiced dirty tricks of "seasoned" players. There are so many dirty plays, and some are quite sophisticated: hand checking, jersey grabbing, elbowing, knee nailing, arm locking, and so forth. They may not always cause injuries, but they are indeed ugly!

Occupational Health and Ergonomics

Basketball is a popular sport, and also a profession for many players. The objective of a sport is to improve the physical condition of participants in order to contribute to healthy living. Nowadays professionals do it for a living, yet they still have the majority of their lives after retirement from competition. Therefore, occupational health and ergonomics are big issues for basketball players of all levels.

✘ The conventional shooting mechanics are a mechanically designed and physically trained process. They **disobey ergonomics**; they are not natural in human kinetics, unrelated to any traditional or genetic inherent human physical activities such as agricultural works or military exercises.

✘ Conventional jump shooting needs **special training** over long periods for muscle buildup and coordination. Other than for shooting the basketball, the built muscle mass is not useful and thus a burden to daily living. It is hard to find the usefulness of basketball shooting posture in daily life, except for perhaps some construction jobs or automobile repair.

✘ Conventional shooting is the main scoring method in basketball games. Players spend most of their training time **practicing jump shots**. Their shooting hands remain unchanged throughout their careers. The muscle masses and powers between the shooting and non-shooting hands are unbalanced. The shooting hand and arm are highly exposed to wear and tear and injuries from overuse.

✘ Injuries are direct physical hazards to players. Most injuries are traumatic, as they occur suddenly from unpredictable incidents during basketball games. They are unavoidable due to body contact and complex and rapid movements.

✘ Basketball involves constant and intensive jumping, running, and cutting. **Overuse injuries** in basketball are caused by repeatedly stressing an area until it is damaged.

The Necessity of a Basketball Revolution

Despite these adversities and challenges we face, basketball is still a beloved sport of youths and fans of all ages, simply because the essential elements of basketball never changed. These elements are run, jump, throw, dribble, pass, and shoot.

For the future of basketball, about which many of us feel passionate, the need for a revolution is imminent. The existing techniques cannot solve their own problems. A technical revolution won't be commenced until some technical breakthrough occurs.

Modern basketball has reached its limit. In technical aspects, basketball, especially professional basketball, can be positively changed and significantly improved with new techniques. They can change fundamental skills—not the essence of the game, but the way the game is played. Now the new techniques are available, and a technical revolution is feasible.

The discovery of Universal Ball-Handling Mechanism and Universal Shooting Mechanism manifests the advent of a technical revolution of basketball. This revolution will bring positive changes to basketball and health benefits to the public. It will improve every aspect of basketball games.

REVOLUTION THEORIES AND MECHANISMS

For the revolution theories, we have all fundamental scientific disciplines, studies, and researches on human physiology and kinetics, and physiodynamics and biomechanics of the human body, particularly in hands and brain study and ergonomics. These studies will be expanded in chapter 2 for specific applications in basketball techniques and skills.

With the scientific foundations, we have three major mechanisms in basketball application:

- *3fz*—Universal Ball-Handling Mechanism
- *UniShot*—Universal Shooting Mechanism
- *4u1*—Universal Alignment

What is *3fz*?

Three-Finger Zen is an integrated skill of ball handling. It is an innate mechanism of one-hand ball control by applying primarily **the last three fingers** (*MAP*: middle finger, annular finger, and pinky) of the hand—*3fz* is a natural process of fingers, hand, and arm movements, as well as coordination within the human body.

This Universal Ball-Handling Mechanism unifies all basketball-handling techniques and skills, namely dribbling, passing, catching, and shooting. In theory, *3fz* mechanism is abstracted as a one-hand-only ball-handling process. The process includes ball catch, ball control, dynamic triple threat, direction change, ball set, twist and spin control, and push, shoot, and release. *UniShot* is a full application of *3fz* mechanism in the process of shooting basketball with the non-shooting hand assistance.

The *4u1* alignment—Universal Alignment is the core of the *3fz* ball-handling mechanism, and it dictates the quality and precision of each step of the one-hand-only process. This alignment is a unique neural and biomechanical connection between thumb and ring finger for precise basketball control. Detailed technical descriptions of *4u1* are given in chapters 2 and 7.

In this book, *3fz* is the prime mechanism of manipulating the basketball; however, it is also applicable to other ball-handling sports: handball, water polo, volleyball, baseball, and shot put.

The mover and shaker of the basketball revolution is *3fz*. It is a technical complex with the following simple concepts:

- **Advanced individual skill.** It applies new techniques to fundamental basketball skills including footwork, dribbling, passing and catching, shooting and rebounding, and moving with and without the ball. Physical conditioning, skill training, and team working of modern basketball are the foundations of *3fz* applications. Retroactively, *3fz* will change the ways of basketball training and conditioning.

- **One for all.** With its unique ball-control mechanism, *4u1*, and shooting mechanism, *UniShot*, *3fz* has the capability of replacing all existing skills (dribbling, passing, and shooting) of basketball offense.

- **Tao of basketball offense.** As an individual skill that changes the team game, *3fz* leads new ways of playing the whole basketball game—offense and defense.

In praxis with *3fz* symmetric training, basketball players can systematically achieve ambidexterity for accurate long shots and passes. On dynamic one-footed or two-footed jumps, *3fz* generates a large variety of moves and shots, and gives offensive players pure technical dominance over single-coverage defense in the perimeters.

- The *3fz* training enhances physical, mental, and intellectual development of youths.
- It stimulates rarely used muscles and nerves associated with the ring and little fingers of the hand, establishes internal learning mechanism between dominant and weak hands (sides, or axes), and sparks interconnections of the logic and intuitive halves of the human brain.
- Conditioning with *3fz* effectively improves players' athletic systems, cognitive skills, and learning abilities.

Generally, *3fz* promotes overall health of the participants of the sport of basketball, and it benefits players of any age and gender, helping their physical and mental well-being.

What is *UniShot*?

Again, *UniShot* stands for Universal Shooting Mechanism, a new basketball shooting technique. It is a natural ball-propelling process that applies *3fz* mechanism in shooting a basketball, as compared to the conventional shot, which uses designed and trained shooting mechanics that are contradictory to human engineering.

Universal Shooting Mechanism is composed of following new ball-controlling techniques:

- *MAP* ball catching
- Finger-Spring Cup (*FSC*) holding
- Reverse-Finger Twist (*RFT*) setting
- *MAP* shooting
- Ring finger releasing

UniShot has ambidextrous up-handed and underhanded shots on one-footed or two-footed jump (or no jump). For up-hand *UniShot*s, there are one-handed and two-handed releases. Chapter 3 *UniShot* gives you detailed technical descriptions.

UniShot works with the following concepts and objectives:

- **A simple, practical shooting technique suitable for everyone** to replace all existing scoring methods: the conventional shots, hooks, layups, dunks, and other forms of shooting throws
- Solve current shooting problems and significantly **increase shooting accuracy and range**
- Inherit the advantages and assets of the existing scoring methods: practical jump shooting posture, hook-shot high protective position, and layup quickness
- Dynamically combine basic movements of human kinetics: running, jumping, throwing, and turning
- Simplify, unify, and standardize the scoring methods of basketball
- Empower shooting with variety, ambidexterity, and protection, and enable *UniShooter*s to dominate single-man defense

Figure 1. Active ball contact area of hand for shooting basketball

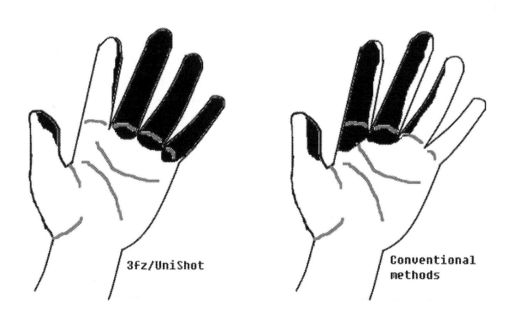

3fz/UniShot

Conventional methods

Technical comparison: conventional shot versus UniShot

(Conventional shooting method: standard two-hand over-the-head square-feet jump shot)

	Conventional Method	*UniShot*
Hand(s) on ball	Two hands	One hand or two hands
Foot (feet) on ground, or jump	Two feet squared	One-footed jump, or two feet squared or scissors
Ball release off	Index finger	Ring finger
Alignment	Middle with elbow-in	Universal
Hand Position	Uniformed	Up-handed and underhanded
Ambidexterity	No	Yes
Variety	Uniformed	Many
Protection	No	Yes
Power	Low	High
Accuracy	High in practice; low on defense	Very high in practice; same on defense

REVOLUTION PROCESS

To eliminate the above obstacles, to solve the current technical problems, and to advance basketball to the next level, we do need a revolution for the perfect basketball game that many of us dream about. A revolution needs fundamental theories, innovative mechanisms and techniques, and good praxes. The praxis here stands for the applications of theories and mechanisms into basketball practice.

Heretofore, we have scientific foundations and revolutionary mechanisms of *3fz* and *UniShot*. What about praxes? How can an average basketball player learn related new techniques and skills? How long does it take to practically apply *3fz* and *UniShot* in competitive games?

Individual Praxis

As a basketball lover for many years, I play the sport, study the game, and at the same time, conduct research on how to improve the game in any innovative way. My education in mechanical engineering and health sciences has been helpful to my basketball endeavors. With my persistent unconventional praxis and constant prayers, I was given a wonderful tool of *3fz* to help people achieve basketball excellence.

Here is the long, hard journey to my discovering *3fz* and *UniShot*. Fortunately, you do not need to follow. This is just for you to know how the road to the treasure was blazed and the *MAP* was made.

- In the summer of 2003, at age forty-seven, I started to work out by practicing basketball regularly, for about two hours a day. Since I had tennis elbow in my right arm, it was hard for

11

me to shoot shots longer than twenty feet (six meters). I had to change my shooting hand to my left hand; as a learning process, I also shot the ball by alternating left and right hands.

- Two years later, I found out that one-handed ambidextrous long shots were almost unchallengeable in one-on-one games. In these shots, I did not use the conventional elbow-in and index-finger-release techniques, and involved more of my ring finger. My defenders were not able to interfere with my shot because my shots were set high on the far side; when they tried to challenge my shots, they had to move to my shooting side and give up their boxing out positions for rebound.

- In 2007, I found *UniShot*, Universal Shooting Mechanism with two-hand shooting set with *RFT*, Reverse-Finger Twist, and all five fingers shooting basketball. I could shoot more accurately because there was more control of ball spin and twist with the ring and little fingers.

- In early 2009, *UniShot* as a prime shooting method was quickly upgraded to *3fz*—Universal Ball-Handling Mechanism, in which Finger-Spring Cup (*FSC*) was established by applying mainly the last three fingers (*MAP*) of hand.

- In the same year, in the integration of *UniShot* and *3fz*, the amazing low-hand *UniShot* was born. *UniShot* is then completed with both up-handed and underhanded shots that are capable of overtaking all the existing scoring methods.

- Finally, in 2010, Universal Alignment (*4u1*) was discovered as the law of one-hand controlling the basketball.

I learned everything by praying to God. It was a long and hard trial of my faith. There were no references, no coaches or teammates, no one understanding—just basketball and me. It was an arduous progression from *UniShot* to *3fz*, and then to *4u1*. But I did find the training methods behind these mechanisms and a short cut for mastering *3fz* and *UniShot*.

The correct and quickest way to a successful revolution is *from 4u1 to 3fz to UniShot*.

1. **Command *4u1* in hand.** It is best achieved with pure physical conditioning by strengthen the ring-finger-to-thumb connection. Then you can do calibration on a basketball in dribbling practice. Gradually, you will have precise *4u1* alignment in your hands, and you will never lose it.

2. Not waiting for the full *4u1* establishment in your hand, you can work on fundamental *3fz* training. **Strengthening your *MAP*** is a continuous conditioning process that requires great patience and persistent effort. The fine muscles associated with ring and little fingers take time to develop in mass, strength, and skill. After you learn to do ***FSC***, you should start right away with **low-hand *UniShot***.

3. **Mastering up-hand *UniShot* is a long-term process.** Combined with *3fz* dribbling, passing, and low-hand *UniShot* training, you will get much faster results than that in my praxis.

Revolutionary Praxes

In the summer of 2010, I spent four months in Taiwan and mainland China, trying to introduce *3fz* and *UniShot* to the basketball experts. Among them are Chinese and American professional coaches, officers of national basketball operations, professors of sports institutions, and professional and college players. The reasons for first introducing *3fz* to China overlapped: (1) In China, I have business connections, and at the same time, I could spend more time with my ailing parents; (2) basketball is extremely popular there, especially with younger generations; (3) children dining with chopsticks might have practice in using their ring fingers. Weird thought? Please read chapter 2 for further explanation.

It was not a successful business trip, as I couldn't get this unconventional way of playing basketball through to the basketball experts to start any training program of *3fz* with their responding basketball teams. In retrospect, I should have put together the contents of this book with detailed technical explanations of everything about *UniShot* and *3fz*.

On the other hand, the trip was hugely successful in terms of revolutionary praxes. I gratefully found three basketball teachers at Zhulin High School in Taipei, Changxing County Sports School, and Beijing Sport University.

In July 2010, I gave six hours of *3fz* training over three days (two hours each day) to the Zhulin High School basketball team. They were boys between the ages of fifteen and seventeen. In these three short sessions, they learned *3fz* fundamentals and were able to use it in handling the basketball. One of the amazing shots they could make, after six hours of practicing *3fz*, was a low-hand *UniShot* five meters away from basket. That was a regular layup jumping from the free throw line, which **professional players cannot do**. And they made a sizzling 60 percent of the shots, almost two out of their three attempts in a media (Taiwan Dong Sen TV News of July 30, 2010) testing. It can be viewed at this web address: http://news.cntv.cn/china/20100730/102928.shtml.

Two weeks later, in Changxing, I trained a group of boys and girls who were twelve to fourteen years old. They had only a total of three hours of training in two days, and they were able to initially command *3fz* fundamentals in controlling the ball. Afterward, Changxing basketball school decided to use *3fz* conditioning as their regular training. In September, I had a chance to introduce *3fz* and *UniShot* to senior students (over twenty years of age) in two classes at Beijing Sport University. In a short two hours of training, half of the students could control the basketball with *3fz* mechanism.

During the past two years, I have occasionally taught a number of adults at their requests, and some of them are established good shooters. After they learned some fundamental *3fz* drills and got the feelings of *MAP* on the ball in their first training, they became more confident in controlling the ball with *3fz* in setting their conventional shooting. That was after just one hour of training!

I spent about four hours playing basketball with my nephew in August 2010. He was sixteen and had virtually **no basketball skill**. In his first five minutes of playing with the ball, I realized that the boy had no body coordination in his shots, and his driving moves were awkward. Actually, he had not shown me any sport talent. His parents, my brother and sister-in-law, did not have athletic skills other than jogging and biking.

The first day, I taught him *3fz* fundamentals, and he was so excited about it being the first time he could grab the ball and handle the ball with *3fz*. The second day, I decided to do an experiment on him by trying every *UniShot*. The boy was so hyper that he did learn almost all the *UniShot*s

(underhanded and up-handed) with good shooting percentage around the basket and in middle ranges. He had no problem in learning any of the *3fz* and *UniShot* techniques!
The 3fz method has not failed! Needless to say, 3fz and UniShot are good for everyone to learn.

I found the treasure, you got the map; I blazed the trial, you follow it!

The simplicity of learning *3fz* lies in the fundamental approaches in training and conditioning. In *3fz* conditioning, the unique way of accessing the resources of our hands leads to basketball excellence.

The shortest and correct route to find your own talents is to do the following:

1. Train *MAP* and get precise *4u1* alignment of hand
2. Command *3fz* mechanism in handling basketball
3. Do low-hand *UniShot*
4. Master all *UniShot*s

In your brain, you need to have a good understanding of your hands and your body, physiologically and biomechanically. With this knowledge, you will learn all these revolutionary basketball skills in a relatively short time. Surely it will be much less time than I spent.

Individual Revolution Plan

This is a two-year plan based on **one to two hours a day, six days a week**, of *3fz* and *UniShot* conditioning and training. The plan should be carried out ambidextrously in *3fz* symmetric training, along with solid theoretical understanding of *3fz* mechanism and its principles.

Time Line	*Milestones*
1st week	Comfortable *MAP* ball control
2nd week	Confident *FSC* formation
3rd week	Fluent *3fz* dribbling
4th week	**Good (>60%),** ambidextrous low-hand *UniShot* from free throw line
6th week	Precise *4u1* alignment for dribble and pass
2 months	Precise *4u1* for low-hand *UniShot*
3 months	**Accurate (>80%),** ambidextrous low-hand *UniShot* from free throw line
	Good, ambidextrous low-hand three-point *UniShot*
4 months	Confident *RFT* clutch
5 months	Good up-hand *UniShot* from free throw line
6 months	Accurate, ambidextrous low-hand three-point *UniShot*
8 months	Precise *4u1* for up-hand *UniShot*
10 months	Accurate up-hand *UniShot* from free throw line
1 year	**Dynamic** (with drives and moves) low-hand three-point *UniShot*s
	Good up-hand three-point *UniShot*
15 months	Good one-foot up-hand three-point *UniShot*
18 months	Accurate up-hand three-point *UniShot*
21 months	Ambidextrous low-hand *UniShot*s with half hooks

2 years   Dynamic, ambidextrous up-hand *UniShot*s with dribble combinations

For professional or college basketball players, this plan can be much shorter, as they train more and train harder. Up-hand *UniShot* techniques can be used as enhancement of your existing shootings until you command *4u1* in your hand. After that, you will be confident in practicing shoot up-hand *UniShot*s; the best time to start the up-handed shooting is during off-season.

The First Amazing Shot!

Mastering *3fz* and *UniShot* takes a lot of practice and quite a bit of time. But one amazing shot that you can do on your own by following my instructions in this book is low-hand one-footed three-point *UniShot*s. That is a three-point layup.

If you specifically practice *3fz* and low-hand *UniShot* for just one hour each day, after three to six days, you will be confident in making it steadily from the free throw line. After a month, you will be able to control your shooting techniques and make the shot constantly. In three months, you will be able to make, with great confidence, **three-point layups** in the game.

Based on my practice and training of teenagers, that is the first *UniShot* that I am sure everyone can learn at an exceptionally fast pace.

Chapter 2

3fz: Three-Finger Zen

As we discussed in chapter 1, *3fz*—Universal Ball-Handling Mechanism—will bring a technical revolution to basketball by changing fundamental skills of offense. It is a newly discovered natural mechanism of our body for handling the basketball. Learning *3fz* requires good understanding of its principles and techniques in order to apply it in each specific skill of basketball offense. The fundamental drills and tips provided in this chapter give you preconditioning to learn and practice basic *3fz* techniques.

By mastering *3fz*, everyone is able to dominate (not just beat) any single defensive coverage (or one-on-one) in a basketball game. If you are an established basketball player, most of your fundamental skills are applicable in upgrading to *3fz*. However, you need to change the concepts of playing and training basketball to the new technical aspects with educated training.

Learning *3fz* is not difficult as long as you have a good understanding of how it works in both theory and praxis. The learning process is more of an intellectual and mental process than a physical one. By applying academic knowledge of physics, mathematics, biology, physiology, and kinesiology into *3fz* praxis, it takes much less time to command *3fz* and related techniques. Keep in mind that *3fz* learning is not a conventional physical skill training, which is attained by tedious repetition. Educated training is the key of *3fz* success.

3fz: UNIVERSAL BALL-HANDLING MECHANISM

Again, *3fz* is a simple, natural mechanism for our hands and arms to manipulate the basketball. It obeys the principles of ergonomics for the most efficient human kinetics, the safest athletic moves and shots, and the healthiest working environments for the players.

It employs primarily *MAP* to control and manipulate a basketball. The thumb and index finger have secondary roles of supporting and guiding the ball. The *3fz* mechanism applies basic principles of human physiology and kinesiology into new techniques.

- By actively involving *MAP*, *3fz* explores more biomechanical and kinetic resources of hand and arm. It fully utilizes the hand's radian stability and **ulna mobility** for maximum ball-manipulating scopes and controlling power in dribbling, passing, and shooting. It also elevates players' offensive skills with exceptional shooting accuracies and ball-control precisions.

- It takes advantages of the hand's **geometrical stability** (hand and finger holding the ball), structured by abducting thumb and *MAP* for secure and smooth one-hand ball controls to catch, lift, fake, twist, throw, and shoot.

- It enhances neural and biomechanical connections between thumb and ring finger and establishes **Universal Alignment** inside hand. The *4u1* alignment ensures a precise positioning of all five fingers on the ball surface, with which *3fz* produces stable, flexible, and precise single-handed ball control.

- **Innate in our hand and arm**, *3fz* is the most efficient mechanism of handling the basketball. Despite its fundamental distinction in finger positioning from the existing ball skills, it can be easily, naturally learned by understanding *3fz* theories, concepts, and processes and practicing accordingly.

- It is **the DNA** of **Universal Shooting Mechanism**, a unique basketball shooting mechanism with dynamic forms, complete protection, and exceptional accuracy. With its multifaceted technical edges, *UniShot* can replace all the existing scoring methods: the conventional shots, hooks, layups, and any other shooting throws.

Chapters 3, 5, and 6 will give detailed technical descriptions, analyses, applications, and procedures of *3fz* and *UniShot*.

Everyone can learn and master *3fz*; it has no special physical or athletic requirements. In order to command *3fz* techniques in a relatively short time, you need to understand more about your body's physiology and biomechanics, especially in the hands. Learning *3fz* is a creative process of intense training of your hands, body, and brain simultaneously.

> Three-Finger Zen is the Tao, the Way, of playing basketball from the grace of God. In His image, men and women were created with two amazing graces, brain and hand, of unlimited resource and capability. Each of our hands has five fingers; each was made special, resourceful, and creative. It is the unique mechanism of handling a round ball. It touches the ball from the tips of five fingers; connects to the brain through each side of the limbs and crossover; naturally coordinates muscles, bones, and nerves; and produces excellent power and control in manipulating the ball.

I first tried to use all five fingers playing basketball; in the processes, the last three fingers—*MAP*—gave more control, power, and dynamics in dribbling and passing the ball. That led me to shoot the ball up-handed and underhanded, with improved accuracy and range. Then I found out that *MAP* is the three primary fingers used to handle a basketball for any skill. With thumb support for Universal Alignment of hand, *3fz* ball-handling mechanism is precise, powerful, and adaptable to all individual and team basketball offenses.

When I perceived the Tao and started to practice it seven years ago, I did not exactly know it. After two years of practice and prayer, I realized that *UniShot* is the way of shooting basketball. As time passed, God finally led me to recognize that the Tao is *3fz*, Universal Ball-Handling Mechanism. It resides right in our hands.

4u1—Universal Alignment

Universal Alignment is the unique ball-control mechanism of the hand, aligned between the tips of the thumb and ring finger via the palm (figure 4). In the process of controlling the basketball, it works in the following ways:

- On catching or holding the ball, the ring finger and thumb form a curve, focusing the center point of the ball, with the open fingertips pressing on the ball at each end of the curve.
- In changing ball-moving directions, the ring finger and thumb curve (*4u1*) keeps its focus at the ball center and applies the middle finger, little finger, and wrist to control the ball's movements.
- On the release, the tip of the ring finger, the ball center, and the target are aligned in the same straight line.

The law of *3fz* one-hand ball control is *4u1*. In handling the basketball, it is universally applicable to all ball skills, adjustable to players' body movements and postures, and independent of ball-moving directions and court positions. The *4u1* principle apples in every hand-ball contact, regardless of whether catching, dribbling, passing, or shooting.

The *4u1* alignment is an innate neural and biomechanical unity of the hand, from the tip of the ring finger through the palm to the distal thumb. Once acquired, *4u1* is static and natural in the hand, never lost. It can be flexibly adjusted in dribbling, passing and shooting. Your dynamic body—elbow, shoulder, hip, knee, ankle, and foot—aligns automatically with the hand's *4u1* in shooting processes. It enables *3fz* to generate the most accurate basketball-shooting mechanism, *UniShot*.

The technical standard of the *3fz* mechanism is *4u1*. Whether you dribble, pass, or shoot the basketball, the key is maintaining *4u1* in your hand from ball catch to final release. Biomechanically, the *4u1*-aligned hand can generate exceptional power and control to direct the ball to intended *dribbling* spot and bounce, optimal *passing* speed and curve, and desired *shooting* arc and spin. With *4u1* in hand, a player can securely and smoothly control the ball with one hand, while the other hand can protect the ball or fend off the defense.

MAP: *Middle Finger, Annular Finger, and Pinky*

The middle finger is the longest finger, right in the middle of the hand, and the second most powerful digit after the thumb. It is the most useful finger in complex human activities such as writing, dining, and artisan works. In sports, the middle finger is the indispensible finger in any hand-involving activities; tipping a volleyball or basketball is an example of the middle finger's extensibility.

The little finger is structurally the shortest finger of the hand. However, with its direct association to ulna mobility and relative independency of other fingers, it has the greatest degree of freedom. There are as many muscles for pinky dynamics as for the thumb: opponent, extensor, and abductor.

The ring finger is the weakest finger of the hand and has the least degree of freedom. It is hard to use the ring finger alone to perform any task other than pressing a piano key. If you try to actively move your ring finger to flex, extend, or abduct, the adjacent fingers move along with it involuntarily.

> In daily life, the ring finger is the least useful among the fingers of the hand. It got the name "ring finger" because people thought it was only useful for wearing a wedding ring. In Chinese, the ring finger is called "no-name finger"; for its lack of usefulness, it did not even deserve a real name.
>
> However, without many people noticing, Chinese folks have used the "no-name finger" to help hold chopsticks for thousands of years. Dining with chopsticks is a complex skill that might take adults years to learn. It is actually not as difficult when you do it the correct way, by supporting the lower chopstick with the "no-name finger." Ring finger support is actually a technical standard of using chopsticks. Otherwise, you may only do hand pronation (palm down) but no supination (palm up) in dining; it would look awkward and leave you hungry.

Figure 2. Hand nerves

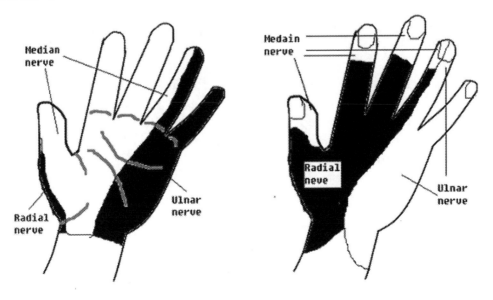

The Nerve System of The Ring Finger

The ring finger has special functions in the human hand. It is about the same length as the index finger and has the same amount of neuron-brain connections as the other four fingers. However, the nerve system of the ring finger is unique. It is the only finger connecting all three nerves—ulna, radian, and median nerves—of the hand and forearm.

1. **The sensory ulna nerve** covers the entire little finger and the ulnar (half) ring finger; **the motor ulna nerve** reaches the intrinsic muscles of all five digits. It makes the ring and little fingers sensitive and flexible to hand dynamics related to ulna mobility.

2. **The median nerve** of the hand covers the palmar thumb, index finger and middle finger, and palmar radial half (to the middle finger) of the ring finger. It makes the ring finger very sensible and reactive to the touches and movements of the first three fingers. The median nerve also establishes strong neural and biomechanical connections between the thumb and ring finger for **Universal Alignment**.

3. **The radian nerve** covers the dorsal wrist and hand, including the entire thumb, index finger, and middle finger, and half of the ring finger. It functions as biomechanical associations of the hand and wrist movements to the ring finger.

For ball handling, there are four direct neural connections starting *from the tip of the ring finger* to the other fingers, hand, and arm.

1. Via the sensory ulna nerve to the little finger, the palmar and dorsal skins around the forth and fifth metacarpals, the ulnar wrist, and the ulnar forearm
2. Via the motor ulna nerve to the intrinsic muscles of the other four digits, the muscles around the fifth metacarpal, ulnar wrist, ulna bone, and associated muscles of forearm
3. Via the median nerve to palmar skins of the first three fingers, palmar wrist integrating radian stability and ulna mobility
4. Via the radian nerve to the dorsal skin of the first three fingers, radial wrist, radian bone, and associated arm muscles

Neurally, the ring finger is *the most sensitive finger* of the hand, and it can instantly act and react with any other finger. When you press your hand against a flat surface such as a table with fully extended and abducted fingers, you can measure the longest distance, between the tips of the ring finger and thumb, that your hand can cover. With its excellent sensibility, mobility, and extensibility, the ring finger can naturally coordinate with the other fingers, especially the thumb, and the wrist and forearm to perform complex tasks. Therefore, the ring finger can be trained as **the information center** and **commander** of the hand, arm, and other coordinating bodies.

Experiment 1. Ring finger sensitivity

By rubbing and pressing your ring finger along the radial palm ridge (palm surface near the middle finger), you will feel heat and pulling inside your thumb from the palm to the tip. If you further press the ring finger backward and toward the little finger (passive extension and abduction), your thumb will respond with a correlative move of abduction, and your palm with a slight pronation. These are the **static neural unity** via the radian nerve, and the **direct biomechanical association** in the hand between the thumb and ring finger.

By rubbing and pressing your ring finger around the ulnar (to little finger) surface, you will feel hot inside the little finger. Then try to actively flex and extend your little finger; your ring finger will moves involuntarily with it. This is the **static and dynamic unity** of the ring finger and little finger, which is directly associated with **ulna mobility**.

Ring Finger Advantages

Besides its unique nerve system, the ring finger has many advantages in sports.

- **It is less likely to be injured.** The ring finger is flexible and must work together with other fingers to perform any task in playing basketball. Rarely has someone jammed or dislocated a ring finger.

- **The ring finger has the least degree of freedom.** In other words, the ring finger must coordinate with other finger(s) in any movements. When you actively use the ring finger for a task, the related finger(s) will follow the ring finger's lead involuntarily.

- **The ring finger is the middle of *MAP*.** The three fingertips form a natural, flexible curve on the ball surface, which can smoothly touch, roll, sweep, twist, and shoot the ball. The ring finger is the center and the pivot of *MAP* in manipulating the ball.

- **The longest shooting lever.** With thumb at pivot, *MAP* can extend to reach the longest distance that a hand can cover. In this leverage (the distance), the shooting forces applied to *MAP* can generate maximum shooting power to the ball.

  The ring finger is relatively weak, but it can be trained to perform complex tasks with greater power and control. For most people, it is hard to learn playing the violin. Probably the hardest part is that a violin player aligns her ring finger to the supporting thumb to reach the farthest positions on the violin panel for high pitches; in this alignment, she can play expressive music with vibrato and harmonics in accurate tones. Biomechanically, it is relatively easy to use the ring finger in *4u1* alignment to control a big, round basketball.

- By focused training for *4u1* establishment in hand, the ring finger can **play commanding roles** in finger adduction/abduction and flexion/extension, thumb flexion/extension and turn, and hand supination/pronation (palm up/down).

Naturally, the ring finger has the capabilities functioning as **the command-and-control center** of all hand and finger movements in handling basketball. Active ring finger involvement and full application of ulna mobility are two pure, dominant technical advantages of *3fz* over the existing basketball skills. The ring finger can be the primary finger in command to coordinate hands, arms, and other body parts in any offensive maneuver with the ball.

21

Ring-Finger-Dominant Sport

A "ring-finger-dominant sport" sounds weird or impossible. But it is a fact in table tennis.

When I learned to play Ping-Pong in 1965, I held the paddle in the upright (penhold) style made famous by Zhuang Ze-Dong, the sole triple (consecutive) table-tennis world champ.

I was never good since I used only my first three fingers to control the paddle. Not until lately did I found out that great penholding table-tennis players, including many world champs, are holding the paddle with the ring finger supporting behind it. With ring finger support, they can use the associated ulna mobility and related muscles, adding more power and dynamics to their plays. It enables wrist deviations and hand pronation and supination, and it generates more swing power and quickness in hitting and spinning the ball.

In the last forty years, the penholding style has shown its technical edges over the fork-holding style by winning the most men's table-tennis world championships. Eventually, the International Table Tennis Federation (ITTF) had to intervene by changing game rules to keep a technical balance between the two styles. They made numerous changes in ball size, weight, and the scoring system, all in favor of the fork-holding style.

Nevertheless, the natural talents are not to be beaten. No matter how the ITTF rules changed, the penholding style, with ring finger techniques, is still winning more world championships. As of this writing, the number one, two, and four world-ranked table-tennis players are the penholders. Wang Hao, the current number one player in the world, has developed a new ring finger technique by hitting backhand in the tennis stoke; this technique will edge out the fork holders in backhanded plays. Technically, the penholders would continue their domination in the sport, because the ring finger gives them more dynamics and variations in playing Ping-Pong.

"If you don't break the egg, it won't stand." Fork holders might have invented table tennis, but penholders revolutionized it. *Now 3fz will revolutionize basketball, making it a ring-finger-dominant sport.*

4u1 Summary

- The *4u1* is a natural finger-aligning mechanism from ring finger to thumb.
- The ring finger is the pivot of *4u1* alignment.
- The ring finger can be trained as information and control center of hand.
- The ring finger is very useful in sports and daily life.
- The *4u1* alignment can be acquired as a permanent skill.

3fz Approaches

The fundamental principles of *3fz* mechanism are based on scientific studies of the human hand and fingers as well as long-term praxes of the most common and efficient hand and arm activities in our daily lives and sports. The objectives of *3fz* are to integrate these theories and praxes in playing basketball, to produce innovative new techniques and skills, and to elevate offense, defense, and the whole game.

Our hands have unlimited capabilities and creativities in sensitive contacts, dynamic movements and descriptive gestures, and powerful grips and twists. All these magic touches are exhibited in excellent performances by musicians with instruments, artisans with tools, and magician with props, and so forth. As we perform hands-on tasks in our daily lives, we all use the same resources innate in our hands.

The tool that is *3fz* facilitates access to the resources of the human hand, unleashing its creativity and capability. It enhances hand-brain communications and enables symmetric developments of limbs. The *3fz* mechanism is an innovative approach in acquiring excellence in sports, full physical and mental development of youths, and health improvement of the general public.

Full Use of Resources

To explore dormant resources of the hand, *3fz* starts from the ring finger, which has long been ignored in basketball, especially in shooting skills. The *3fz* mechanism handles basketball the same way for offense skills of dribbling, passing, and shooting. It catches the ball with *MAP*, controls it in Finger-Spring Cup (*FSC*), shoots (or passes or dribbles) out by *MAP*, and releases it off the ring finger.

The thumb to ring finger alignment (*4u1*) is the technical standard of *3fz* ball handling. It dictates *FSC* formations and smooth *3fz* executions in offensive skills. The quality of *4u1* is the key to fluent dribbling and accurate passing and shooting.

The MAP to Treasures

The ring finger is the entry point of the MAP to the new treasures. From *4u1* to *3fz* is the path of an intellectual, spiritual and physical exploration, from hand to brain; along the path deposit the treasures—natural talents for handling the basketball. *MAP* is the compass of the MAP to find the treasures. You will be rewarded if you follow the MAP and get to the path; the treasures are right in you!

Application Development of Hand Functionality

The *3fz* mechanism develops **a unified offensive skill** that maximizes players' basketball-handling abilities by fully applying hand functionalities: senses, touches, movements, and coordination.

Ulna mobility is a key feature that *3fz* employs, which is not involved in the conventional shooting mechanics. It enables hand supination and pronation; gives flexibility to *MAP*, wrist, and forearm; and generates dynamic powers in throwing or shooting a basketball.

The *3fz* mechanism involves most hand and wrist movements: radial and ulnar deviations of wrist, flexion/extension and adduction/abduction of fingers, and supination/pronation and grips of hand. It actively coordinates hand structures: five digital rays and three ligament arches.

For further details, please refer to the "Biomechanics" section of this chapter.

Symmetric Training for Ambidexterity

Basketball is an ambidextrous sport. Most players have balanced skills between left and right hands in dribbling, passing, and layups. Many big post players can shoot hooks around the basket with either hand. But for the conventional shooting method, it is not necessary or advantageous to use the weak hand to shoot the basketball, as the shooting posture and releasing position remain unchanged anyway.

The *3fz*-driven *UniShot* generates **three-dimensional** shots that can be launched from any position in the scope of hand reach, while the conventional shooting is only one-dimensional in which the body axis, the ball, and the rim must be kept in a direct line (a bit curved but still one dimension). *UniShot* enables one-handed ambidextrous shootings that give offense tremendous advantages. Undergoing *3fz* symmetric training enables the weak hand to acquire systematically the shooting skills from the dominant hand. In the fundamental process of mirror learning (dynamic image copy), *3fz* mechanism generates sensitive touches and precise memories in fine muscles and ligaments of the leading hand, which are transferred to the learning hand through logical thinking of the mind.

A cohesive learning process between the left hand-right brain axis and the right hand-left brain axis, *3fz* cross-connect symmetric training enables players to learn ambidextrous *UniShot*s with great simplicity. Contralateral (cross-axial) mirror learning is the key process of the symmetric training; it accelerates the learning by active exchanges of brain and muscle memories between teaching and learning body axes. Detailed technical descriptions are included in chapter 7.

Hand and Brain Connections for Physical and Mental Health

Playing the piano is an excellent exercise of stimulating brain activity with the movement of the fingers on the keyboard. Harmonized with classic music, it enhances the physical and mental developments of young people. This enhancement is referred to as the "Mozart effect."

Human hand and finger biomechanics and on-ball praxis are the main subjects of implementing the *3fz* mechanism for basketball. There are two basic hand and finger activities on the basketball: **finger perception** for ball touch and **hand manipulation** for ball control. In *3fz* basketball practice, you work with rhythmic ball bounces and creative body movements. The effects of the hand-body-mind connecting practices are better than the Mozart effect because you involve your whole body and the movements are symmetric.

With its innovative approaches, *3fz* cross-connect symmetric training actively merges **two contralaterally associated axes**: right hand to left (logic thinking) brain and left hand to right (intuitive thinking) brain associations. In the merge process, our brains, hands, and bodies work together in dynamic yet harmonized inner and outer environments. Both axes of brains and limbs will interact with each other to learn and improve dramatically. This kind of training will benefit players with greater athletic ability, mental acuity, memory capacity, and logic and intuitive talents.

Unified Basketball Skill and Training

Use of *3fz* leads to the standardization of basketball offense. Its objective is to have one simple, effective, and powerful mechanism to handle (dribble, pass, and shoot) the basketball in any game setting. The offensive skills will be unified and trained in the same way. The level of ball-handling skills will be solely dependent on the qualities of mastering *3fz*.

This natural, simplified and unified ball-handling mechanism will bring significant improvements in shooting variety and accuracy, passing abilities, and dribbling proficiency. The *3fz* mechanism lowers the physical requirements of basketball players, changes the conventional way of training, alters the courses of team offense, and positively affects the defense and the whole game.

HAND ANATOMY

Handling a basketball is about building harmony between ball and hand. With that in mind, we first need to know our ball touching and manipulating hand and how it works.

Figure 3. Hand anatomy

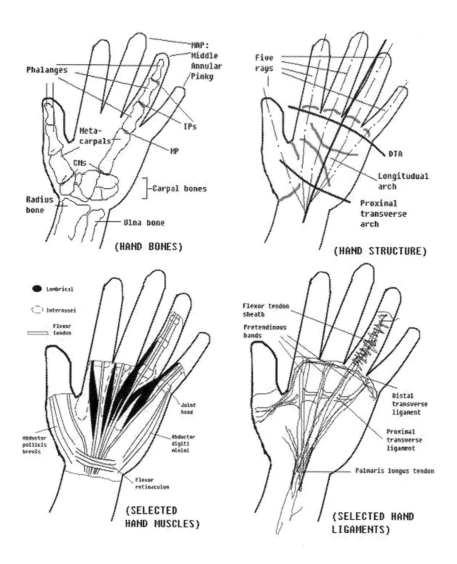

Bone Structure of Hand

Starting from fingertips, a hand has fourteen phalanges (finger bones, two for thumb and three for each of the other four fingers), five metacarpals (palm bones connecting finger bones), and eight carpal bones (wrist bones). The carpal bones are made up of two rows of four bones, bridged by flexor retinaculum (wrist-covering ligaments) that forms the carpal tunnel. There are fifteen major joints of the fingers, and there are more movable surface among the carpal bones and wrist joints.

Major Hand and Wrist Joints

- **Carpal joint.** The carpal joint, the wrist joint, is made up of many different joints. The ends of the radius and ulna bones and eight carpal bones form these joints. The distal radioulna joint, the radiocarpal joint, the ulnocarpal joint, the midcarpal joints, and the carpal-metacarpal (CM) joints comprise the wrist joint.

The distal radioulna joint allows the wrist and arm movements of pronation and supination. Supination is rotation of the forearm for palming up and pronation for palming down.

Functionally, the joints of the wrist work together to allow the wrist to bend for wrist flexion, straighten for wrist extension, and turn inward with ulnar deviation and outward with radial deviation.

- **Metacarpophalangeal (MP) joints.** There are five MP joints in hand jointing palm and fingers. They roll and glide in the same directions, forward with flexion and backward with extension.

- **Interphalangeal (IP) joints.** There are nine finger IP joints, one for the thumb and two for the other four fingers, supported by two collateral ligaments and small volar plates.

Muscles, Tendons, and Ligaments

Hand muscles have small masses and lengths but with complex structures. They coordinate ligaments, joints, and bones for hand and finger movements. Functionally, they are thenar (thumb muscles), hypothenar (little finger muscles), adductor pollicis (muscles to close fingers), interosses (palm muscles between metacarpals), and lumbricals (inner muscle for finger flexion and extension). They have origins and insertions within the hand bones.

Nine extensor tendons course from the dorsal forearm of the wrist and hand. The extensor digitorum communis—common finger extensor—tendons are jointed distally near the MP joints by fibrous interconnections called juncturae tendinum—juncture tendons.

Nine flexor tendons course over the volar forearm, wrist, and hand and pass through the carpal tunnel.

The flexor retinaculum is a thickening of deep fascia (connecting tissue) attached to the inside of carpal bones. Palmar aponeurosis is fascia of the palm.

Three Nerves

- **The ulna nerve** is the major motor sensor of the hand and controls hypothenar muscles, interosses, third and fourth lumbricals, flexor pollicis brevis, and adductor pollicis; the superficial branch of the ulna nerve covers the skin of the hypothenar, the little finger, and the ulnar half of the ring finger.

- **The median nerve** reaches the thenar and the first and second lumbricals. It covers the skins of the thenar, the central part of the palm, the palmar index finger and middle finger, the radial-palmar ring finger, the dorsal-distal index finger and middle finger, and the dorsal-distal-radial ring finger.

- **The radian nerve** covers the dorsal-proximal skins of the index finger and middle finger, the dorsal-proximal-radial skin of the ring finger, and the dorsal thumb.

HAND GEOMETRY

Hand size is important in handling the basketball. Possessing the same skill as a smaller hand, a bigger hand has more coverage on the ball and more stable and secure control than a smaller hand does. Children develop bigger hands as they grow, and their basketball skills likewise advance. For adults, it is important to understand our hands' geometrical dimensions and to use them wisely in sports.

The conventional shooting emphasizes ball control with the radian tripod formed by the first three fingers: thumb, index finger, and middle finger. This structure is vertically stable but lacks horizontal stability with its small control area on the ball; it is inflexible with no dynamic ulna associations.

Hand Coverage

By pressing the hand with fully abducted fingers on a flat surface, we can measure the area of hand coverage.

- The hand coverage is about a round area with a diameter of ring finger to thumb.
- The tip-to-tip distances from thumb to middle finger, to ring finger, and to little finger are about the same.
- The shortest measurement is the distance between thumb and index finger.
- The radial tripod covers less than half area of hand coverage.
- *MAP* and thumb forms a stable spherical isosceles triangle with ring finger to thumb as the height, and thumb, middle finger and little finger as the corners of the triangle.

This is also the hand coverage on a basketball when you grab the ball the same way. If we use the thumb tip as a supporting point, the longest distance is the height of the isosceles triangle, about the same distance of the thumb to the tips of *MAP*. Universal Alignment is precisely calibrated along this longest arm to apply shooting forces of *MAP* generated by the whole body. In high school physics, the torque (moment) is the production of applying force and applied distance, which is expressed as:

$$P = F \times L$$

P—shooting torque
F—shooting force on *MAP*, generated by the whole body
L—distance (length) of the arm of the shooting force

Figure 4. Arms of shooting forces

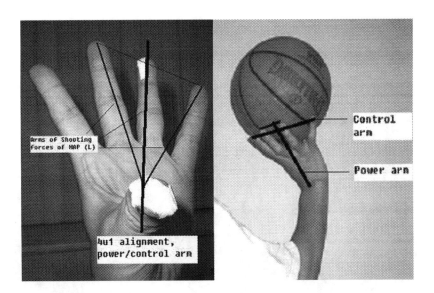

From the equation above, one can generate maximum shooting power with applied force of the body to the longest moment arm. In the same hand coverage, we can also have stable shooting control with *MAP* involvements.

Experiment 2. Everybody can grab a full-size basketball, no matter how small one's hand is!

Put the ball on a soft place, perhaps on your lap when you sit, but not on your hand. Hold down the ball on top with open palm and relaxed fingers. Twist the ball in radial deviations, turning wrist inward (counterclockwise if with right hand) for full turns of your wrist. Do it for several twists until you feel that your fingers are warm. Then twist and press the ball down with relaxed open fingers without palm contacting the ball.

Attention! While twisting, point your index finger into the air. Keep twisting the ball with relaxingly flexed *MAP* and thumb. Now try to grab the ball with the four fingertips while twisting. If you can suck up the ball momentarily, that's a good sign. Keep trying it until you can steadily grab it. You will be feeling that you have better and better grips on the ball when you practice this way.

Tip: If your hand is small, try to press your *MAP* fingertips along the seams of the basketball and grab it. If you can't grab the ball the first day, don't worry. Keep trying and the next day you will be much better off. You can surely do it!

Static Finger-Spring Cup (*FSC*) Formation

You don't need to grab the ball to control it with one hand. You can lean your index finger's ulnar (to middle finger) surface to the ball for supporting and guiding purpose, and this way your hand forms an *FSC*—Finger-Spring Cup—to hold the ball in the air one-handed (figure 5).

Figure 5. *FSC*

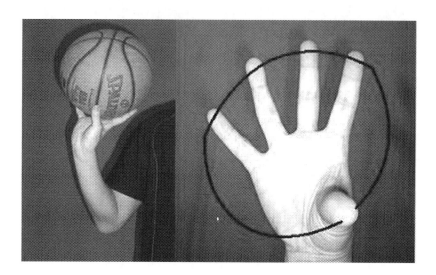

The addition of the index finger gives an extra control area of *FSC* on the ball with three added functions:

1) Supporting the ball in transition of triple threat
2) Guiding the ball in releases
3) Twisting and rolling the ball for layups or passes

FSC sets fingers as spring claws spread evenly on the ball for solid one-handed control. It is more stable while *FSC* is holding underneath the basketball. The sizes of *FSC* are variable depending on the adduction of thumb. The closer thumb leans to the palm, the smaller the size of *FSC* and the longer shooting lever from the wrist.

Hand Sizes

The hand sizes of basketball players vary, of course. It is not necessary that the bigger hands control the ball better. Ball-handling skills are totally dependent on a player's natural talents and training. It is desirable for skilled small hands to have larger control area on the ball. The *3fz* mechanism makes it possible for smaller hands to grab a basketball, and it can also condition the hand to gain more muscle mass to be wider, fatter and stronger.

The length of one's hand remains unchanged after full physical development. However, the width of the hand can be increased with special conditioning. Thinking of traditional barefoot fishermen, their feet were usually flat with wide-open toes. By spending long periods working on boats barefooted, their feet became significantly wider than those of the fishermen who wore shoes.

There are many examples of practiced big and strong hands in history, such as Rachmanonov's hands with the piano, Michelangelo's with chisel, hammer, and paintbrush, and Genghis Khan's with bow and arrow. Today's professional tennis players have strong and relatively big hands because they practice with heavy rackets. I once had a chance to shake hands with Michael Chang, a former Grand Slam champion ranked number two in the world. It was impressive that his hand was solidly firm and fairly large in relation to his relatively small stature as a professional tennis player.

Again, while the bones of a human hand are fixed in length after a certain age, the muscles and ligaments of the palm, between the metacarpals, can be worked for more mass and extensibility. The following are factors contributing to a wider, stronger hand with *3fz* training:

- The distal transverse arch is flexible, powerful, and extensible. It will get more dynamics and power with *3fz* training.
- Thenar and hypothenar can be conditioned for more muscle mass to increase thickness and width of palm.
- Interosses, lumbricals, and other intrinsic muscles can be worked with more extensibility and strength.

You can add index to form an extra ball-controlling area. The distance from the index finger to the little finger is longer than that from the middle finger, and it gives bigger leverage for hand to twist the ball in finger rolls. However, the force applied by the index finger would make the stable isosceles unbalanced and therefore compromise *4u1* alignment. So apply force to the index finger only in ball twists.

BIOMECHANICS OF THE HAND

To explore our hands' resources, we need to know their components and their structures and functions—and more importantly, we should understand their functionalities and how they work together for different movements.

The human hand has twenty-seven bones, thirty-nine muscles, and thirty-six joints. Their arrangements enable hand stability and mobility. The ligaments and intrinsic and extrinsic muscles establish structure and organization, and they generate power and dynamics of hand and finger movements.

Hand and Wrist Structures

Structurally, your hand has five rays and three arches. The five rays are the longitudinal arrays of the metacarpals and phalanges for each of the five fingers. The three arches are the dynamic distal transverse arch, the longitudinal arch, and the relatively stable proximal transverse arch—the carpal arch.

Five Rays

- **The first ray is unique in its structure and mobility.** The first ray consists of two thumb phalanges and the first metacarpal. It is relatively independent in movements of adduction/abduction and opposition to the fifth ray.

- **The five rays have different degrees of mobility and independence.** At the carpometacarpal (CM) articulation, the first and fifth rays have the greatest mobility, the fourth has some, and the second and third rays are relatively fixed.

- **The five rays function differently in grip/pinch.** The two ulnar rays (the fourth and fifth rays) act in palmar grip for support and static control. The three radial rays (the first, second, and third rays) act for precision grip (like key grip) and dynamic control, though the third ray can be integrated with the ulnar rays in power grip (like tennis grip).

Three Arches

The three arches balance stability and mobility of the hand. The proximal transverse arch is rigid, while the other two arches, the distal transverse arch and the longitudinal arch, are flexible, and they are maintained by the hand's intrinsic muscles.

- **Proximal transverse arch.** The carpal arch, a relatively fixed arch, remains arched even when the hand is open.

- **Distal transverse arch (DTA).** It is the metacarpal arch, and it is formed by the metacarpal heads bound together by the deep transverse metacarpal ligaments connecting the volar plates of each MP articulation. The second and third metacarpals are stable with their radian association, while the fourth and fifth metacarpals are relatively mobile with ulna association. This is a mobile arch; the first, fourth, and fifth metacarpals rotate around the second and third metacarpals to either flatten or increase its arc.

- **Longitudinal arch.** Combining the second, third, fourth, and fifth digital rays, the longitudinal arch spans from the fixed CM articulations of proximal transverse arch to the mobile digits, with the MP articulations as keystone support in the middle.

Hand Dynamics

There are two categories of hand movements—perception and manipulation. Perception is the feelings of the hand, which could be active by touching an object or passive if interfacing with the environments. Haptic perception (recognizing through touch) is the contact feelings through the hand, based on tactile and somatosensory (active and passive sensing) information. Manipulation is the hand acting in different movements by coordinating intrinsic and extrinsic muscles or through the mechanisms of the tendons. The following are major dynamic actions of the hand.

- **Grasps.** Without the assistance of wrists and arms, our hands can only do grasps. There are static power grips and dynamic prehensions (precision grasps). In static power grips, the adductor pollicis stabilizes an object in the palm. These types of static grasps include cylindrical (tennis grip), spherical (ball grab), and hook (no thumb) grips. In precision grasps, the hand's position is dynamic, which include tripod grips, tip-to-tip grips, and lateral prehension like key grip.

- **Adduction, abduction, and opposition.** Adduction is the movement of two adjacent parallel parts (e.g., fingers) to get closer to each other. Abduction is the opposite of adduction. Opposition is the turning movement of two surfaces to face each other.

- **Supination and pronation.** Pronation is a coordinated movement of hand, wrist, and forearm by crossing the radius over the ulna. It is a rotation of the forearm from an anterior-facing position to a posterior-facing position, or palm facing down (turning backward). Supination is the opposite movement of pronation, a rotation of the forearm, facing the front or palm up.

- **Radial deviation and ulnar deviation.** Ulnar deviation is the adduction of the wrist, a hand-waving rotation toward the ulna bone. Radial deviation is the abduction of the wrist, the opposite movement of ulnar deviation.

- **Wrist flexion and extension.** There are active wrist flexion and extension by coordinating hand and forearm muscles, and passive wrist flexion and extension by applying external forces on the hand.

- **Finger flexion and extension.** They are the cooperative actions of the palm and finger muscles, with specific mechanisms that will be explained in the next section.

Figure 6. Hand dynamics

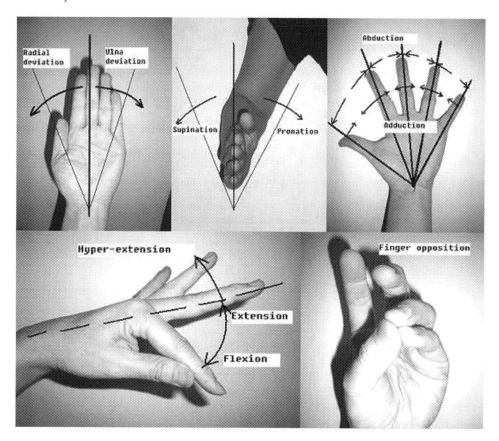

Two Prime Mechanisms of Fingers

Mechanism for finger flexion. Flexor digitorum profundus (FDP) and flexor digitorum superficialis (FDS) coordinate finger flexion. FDP is deeper but has more distal attachments after the proximal IP joint.

Mechanism for finger extension. Finger extensions are coordinated actions of extrinsic and intrinsic extensor muscles. Their primary function is to extend the MP and IP joints. The intrinsic muscles of the hand are the lumbrical and interosseous muscles. They function to extend the IP joints and help flex the MP joint.

- These groups of extrinsic and intrinsic muscles are coordinated by a series of stabilizing retinacular (fibrous connecting tissues) structures, which facilitate balanced transmission of muscular forces. These structures are found in the back of the wrist (extensor retinaculum), the hand (intertendinous connections), and the fingers (extensor hood).

- The extensor mechanism includes expansion, assembly, apparatus, dorsal aponeurosis (fine tendinous layer), and aponeurotic sleeve.

- The extensor mechanism is an elaboration of the extensor digitorum tendon (EDT) on the dorsum of each phalanx. The extensor indicis and the extensor digiti minimi insert into the extensor mechanisms of the second to fifth digits, respectively.

Several tendinous structures comprise the extensor mechanics:

Figure 7. Extensor mechanism and associated hand muscles

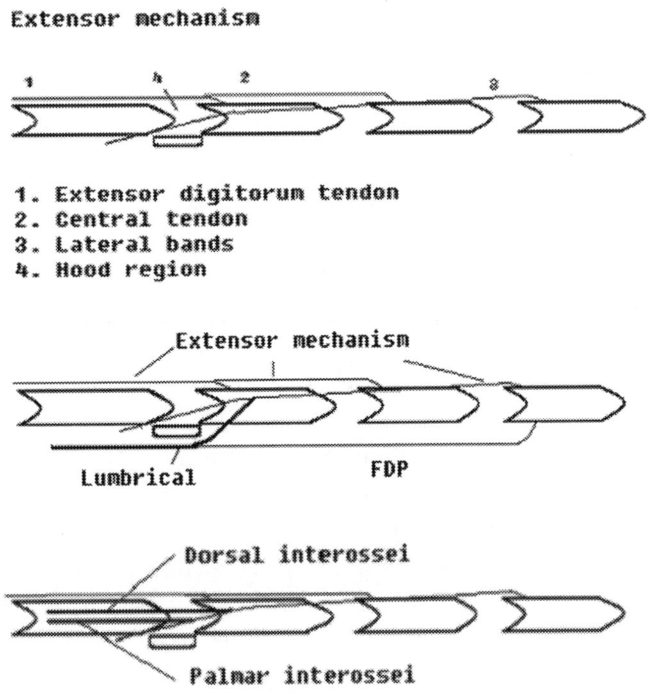

Extensor mechanism

```
1. Extensor digitorum tendon
2. Central tendon
3. Lateral bands
4. Hood region
```

1) **EDT tendon** attaches to proximal phalanx by a tendinous slip, through which MP joint is extended.
2) **Central tendon** applies tension dorsally to the base of middle phalanx and extends the proximal IP joint.
3) **Lateral bands** proceed on the extensor hood and extend the distal IP joint.
4) **Extensor hood** is composed of retinacular and triangular ligaments, which surround MP joint laterally, medially, and dorsally, and receive tendinous fibers from the lumbricals and interossei.

Muscles that transmit force to the otherwise noncontractile extensor mechanism:

- **Dorsal interossei (DI).** Three DIs attach proximally between adjacent metacarpals and distally either to bones (proximal phalanx) or to soft tissues (extensor mechanism). DI produces MP abduction and flexion, and proximal and distal IP extensions, by attaching to the extensor mechanism.

- **Palmar interossei (PI).** Four PIs attach proximally to a metacarpal and distally to the same digit's proximal phalanx and/or its extensor mechanism. They produce MP adduction and flexion, and proximal and distal IP extensions, by introducing tension into the extensor mechanism.

- **Lumbricals.** The four lumbricals attach proximally to the tendons of FDP and distally to the extensor mechanism on its radial side at the level of the lateral bands. The muscles pass on the volar side of the transverse metacarpal ligament. Acting alone, they only produce MP flexion. They also produce proximal and distal IP extensions when they introduce tension into the extensor mechanism.

The lumbricals permit a dynamic interaction between flexors and extensors. Their attachments transmit forces to both the FDP tendon and the extensor mechanism. Specifically, lumbrical activity increases passive tension in the extensor mechanism and decreases passive tension in FDP's distal portion.

Biomechanics of Extensor and Flexor Mechanisms

The tendinous fibers of the extensor mechanism are incapable of producing active force and still transmit forces to their attachments. Forces develop in the extensor mechanism in two ways:

1) The hand's intrinsic muscles, attaching to the extensor mechanism, produce forces that the extensor mechanism communicates to its distal attachments.
2) The extens or mechanism develops passive tension whenever it is elongated by hand activity. This passive tension produces force to its attached structure and the extensor mechanism itself.

The extensor mechanism's fibers have lines of application that are always dorsal to the lateral axis of the proximal and distal IP joints. Therefore, activity in the intrinsic muscles that attach to the extensor mechanism always produces proximal and distal IP extensions. Passive flexion of the MP joint elongates the extensor mechanism and extends the IP joints.

The fibrous lines of application in the hood and lateral bands pass near the MP joint's lateral axis. Whether these structures move the MP joint in the sagittal plane depends on whether the MP joint is already flexed or extended.

MP flexion occurs when activity in the FDS or FDP flexes the MP joint. When the digits flex (at the MP or IP joints), passive tension in the lateral bands and central slip pull the hood distally. When the MP joint is already flexed, the lines of application of the interossei fall on the volar side of the MP joint, producing MP flexion. The distal shift in the extensor hood also increases the lumbricals' moment arms so they can produce a greater flexor moment at the MP joint.

In MP extension, action in the extensor digitorum extends the MP joint and pulls the extensor mechanism (including the hood) proximally. In this position, the interosseous muscles' lines of application are close to the MP joint's lateral axis. With such small movement arms, these muscles have little effect on the MP joint movement in the sagittal plane. However, they still produce MP abduction/adduction when the MP joint is extended.

3fz BIOMECHANICS

The *3fz* is an integrated mechanism of hand and finger movements for handling the basketball. It naturally coordinates hand muscles and bones and their structures in all movements.

Structural Integration

The five digital rays are uniquely organized in Finger-Spring Cup (*FSC*) and Reverse-Finger Twist (*RFT*) as five elastic paws to clutch the ball.

- The *3fz* mechanism takes advantage of the first ray's stability for solid support of the ball as a fulcrum of the force arm in *4u1* alignment.
- It employs the increased flexibilities of the second to fifth rays in smooth ball control in lifting, twisting, swinging, flipping, and wrist joint shaking.
- The *3fz* mechanism involves the hand dynamics, including wrist and finger extension and flexion, ulnar and radial deviations, hand pronation and supination, and adduction and abduction between the rays.

Three arches are dynamically coordinated for optimal ball-holding positions in the hand *FSC* of *3fz* ball-handling mechanism.

- The flexible DTA enables dynamic adjustments of the fingertips for precise finger positioning of the *4u1* alignment.
- The longitudinal arch is twistable to fully employ ulna mobility with the flexible third, fourth, and fifth rays.
- The DTA and longitudinal arches work together with the back-extended wrist to generate more elastic shooting power.
- The relatively fixed proximal transverse arch is frequently pressed by *3fz*'s *FSC* with *RFT* for more power and flexibility in its CM articulations, especially the first, fourth, and fifth CM joints.

Three nerves. In *3fz* mechanism, the ring finger, with its unique connections with all three nerves of the hand, is the communication center.

- By enacting the ring finger as the commander in ball handling, the thumb aligns with it, instantly following the median nerve signals through the palm for precise *4u1* alignment.
- Deep motor branch of the ulna nerves sends instructions from the ring finger to the PIs and lumbricals to coordinate the other three fingers in *FSC* formation.
- In *RFT* clutch, the ulna and median nerves work together to transfer messages from the *MAP* fingertips pivoted at the ring finger, to coordinate the wrist and arm in pronation and

ulnar deviation, and to position the fingers precisely on the ball surface for the shooting *4u1*.

- The radian nerve sends signals, according to feedback from the ring finger, to the wrist and forearm in the back-extension process for maximum shooting power.

3fz Dynamics

The *3fz* mechanism is an integrated process of natural, dynamic movements of the human hand. The ulna mobility is the prime hand resource that *3fz* explores. With direct ulna associations, *MAP* plays a major role in catching, rolling, and shooting the ball. It involves the major movements of hand supination and pronation as well as wrist extension, flexion, and deviations.

In ball-handling processes, *3fz* fully employs flexibilities of the DTA and the longitudinal arch in the prehensions and power grips, in which fingers twist, roll, or sweep the ball. Radial and ulnar deviations are frequent maneuvers of *3fz* dribbling and passing. By *MAP* controlling the ball, finger extension, flexion, and adduction and abduction are the fundamental finger activities of *3fz* mechanism.

Elastic Force and Spring Power

Elastic force, by *3fz* definition, is the force produced in dynamics of the body's joints, in extended forms of the tendons and ligaments associated with joint movements, without contracting major muscles. **Spring power** is generated by applying elastic force to hands or feet.

As with the extensor mechanism, when tendons and their related structures are passively deformed, elastic forces are generated by extraction of the tendons and connected ligaments. The elastic forces are produced in passive flexion or extension of the joints, such as in relaxed skipping-rope jumps. These joints are major joints of contralateral shooting-axis (a shooting hand to the opposite foot) or lateral shooting side (right hand to right foot, or left hand to left foot) of *3fz*-driven *UniShot*s. They include hand joints and elbow, spine, hip, knee, ankle, and foot joints.

In relaxed states, major joints of the body are adjustable in cross-sectional turnings or lateral rotations. For example, in *3fz* shooting set, the wrist is fully back extended by the non-shooting hand pressing the ball, but it can still turn for radial or ulnar deviations. Another example: when your ankle is in passive dorsiflexion at the pressure of your body, you foot can still do inversion or eversion with a slight spin.

The purposes of using elastic forces are the following:

1. Calibrate or adjust *3fz* mechanism of bodies
2. Set the body in dynamic shooting or driving stances or postures
3. Easy adjustment of *UniShot*'s body-shooting alignments
4. Put the body in good static or dynamic balances
5. Integrate elastic forces of joints and ligaments by adjusting limbs for maximal spring power
6. Perform joint-shaking actions or active-reflex ball controls
7. Dynamically apply muscle forces in related mechanisms for controlled shooting powers

The spring power is released from the hand by pushing feet or jumping. They are natural, dynamic powers generated in *UniShot*, producing accurate body-shooting alignments. With spring power and balanced body, you will be able to launch accurate long-range shots every time, effortlessly.

Joint Shaking and Active Reflex

Joint shaking is a voluntary jerk, coordinated actions of joints and ligaments by applying elastic forces. Sports such as fencing and martial arts widely use these kinds of movements or techniques in competitions. By taking advantage of the body's spring powers, the *3fz* mechanism makes full use of joint shaking in the ball-handling processes of passing, dribbling, and shooting, for individual procedures including catching, setting, faking, twisting, flipping, turning, and releasing.

Combined with active reflex, players can apply joint-shake mechanisms in many key basketball executions such as joint-shaking release, dynamic triple threat, pump fake, deceptive passes, and so on. The combination of joint shaking and active reflex is powerful in offensive moves without the ball. A player can initiate body contact with her defender and then make a joint-shaking turn to spring to the opposite direction. This combination makes it hard for the defense to stop players with *3fz* and *UniShot* skills.

Ulna Roll

Ulna mobility is primary functionality of the hand and arm that *3fz* explores. Ulna roll is an integrated *3fz* application of elastic forces/spring power, joint shaking/active reflex, and ulna mobility as a fundamental mechanism of dynamic power generation in *3fz* ball-handling skills. Ulna roll is performed by manipulating the ball on back-extended *MAP* of *FSC* in maximum hand and forearm movements of supination/pronation and DTA twisting.

In Universal Shooting Mechanism, ulna roll is an enhancement in the shooting process for more power and control. With ulna roll, *3fz* can take full advantages of the body's spring power for shooting and passing. It will produce exceptional shooting and passing accuracies and distance. Ulna roll is also the key technique of *4u1* release for *UniShot*s, as a technical standard for advanced shooting releases of *3fz* mechanism.

Ulna roll conditioning and training are stated in chapter 7 *3fz/UniShot* Conditioning and Training.

Ergonomics

With its ambidextrous capabilities, *3fz* actively involves the components and structures of both hands by continuously changing their movements and mechanisms and alternating hands. It is nonrepetitive and generates zero stress to any particular muscle or ligament. In practice, *3fz* mechanism applies mainly elastic forces of joints and tendons; therefore, there is no wear and tear or overuse of muscles and ligaments when players are not competing.

The round basketball, with its relatively soft surface, passively produces even forces to fingers. In *3fz* ball handling, ball touches are gentle and smooth with *MAP*'s flexibility, and it is less likely to have shock forces to jam the fingers. Compared to playing piano with repetitive finger tapping on hard key surfaces, basketball dribbling actions are less likely to result in wear and tear injuries.

Comparing to the existing ball skills, *3fz* utilizes substantially more hand resources by exploring the ring and little fingers' functionalities and taking full advantages of ulna mobility and wrist deviations. *MAP* is the bridge for players to use their conventional skills to learn and advance to *3fz* mechanism. By amplifying finger actions in various combinations, *3fz* simplifies the learning process of the weak hand from the strong hand. The *3fz* symmetric training eliminates stressful drills such as conventional one-stroke-only shooting practice.

The *3fz* mechanism's conditioning stimulates the hand's intrinsic and extrinsic muscles associated with the ring and little fingers, also explores and utilizes ulna mobility, wrist deviations, and other hand movements in handling the basketball. It results in exponential increase in hand ability by cultivating its own resources with smart muscles movements and coordination. The *3fz* symmetric training spikes hand-brain-limb interactivities for elevated physical, mental, and intellectual development of young people. It will also benefit the public in their physical and mental wellness.

3fz TECHNIQUES

Universal Ball-Handling Mechanism comprises three major processes: **catching**, **holding**, and **releasing**. The major technical components of the *3fz* mechanism are ***MAP* ball catch**, ***4u1* alignment**, ***FSC* formation**, and ***MAP* release**.

The following sections are the procedures for applying *3fz* technical components in the ball-handling processes.

Catching Process

Figure 8. Catch a bouncing basketball

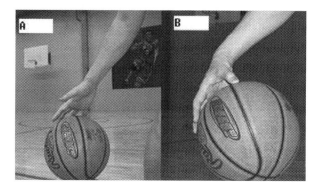

1. *MAP* of the catching hand actively meets the ball with straight arm (with slightly flexed elbow) in the lowest ball-receiving point to the floor (figure 8-A).

2. The *MAP* fingertips first touch and passively poke the up-bouncing basketball on its outside surface, and then actively flex the fingers and roll the ball up into a spherical controlling area under *MAP* to its MP joints.

3. Add the index finger to contact the ball with its ulnar side and to help hold the ball momentarily. Then roll the ball back to the *MAP* fingertips and turn the wrist up with a short radial deviation.

4. Thumb meets the ball passively by touching the ball gently with the radial side to distal phalanx bone at IP joint.

5. Carry the ball momentarily in a horizontal movement to adjust thumb position on the ball by twisting *MAP* pivoting at ring finger to form an *FSC*.

6. Roll the ball up on the supporting thumb along the upper curve of tip and coordinate the *MAP* fingertips with a static twist (figure 8-B).

7. Temporarily sucking holds the ball for triple threat actions. This is a dynamic triple threat point as opposed to the conventional static triple threat position.

8. At the triple threat point, an initial *4u1* from the ring finger's radial side to the thumb is established.

Holding/Control Process

Figure 9. Ball holding with *FSC* and *RFT*

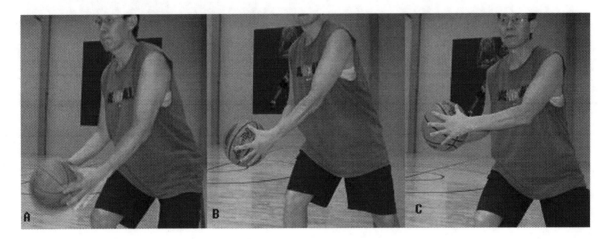

1. After *FSC* is formed and a triple threat *4u1* is established on the catching hand, swing the other hand to clutch the ball at the cup (figure 9-A).

2. Press the ball with the other hand's *MAP* on the ball surface opposite to the catching *FSC* coverage.

3. Twist the ball reversely by the two hands in a form of automobile clutch, with two *FSCs* (as two discs of the clutch) on both sides of the basketball, the catching hand with a radial deviation and the other with an ulnar deviation. This is an *RFT* clutch action (figure 9-B).

4. Lift the ball in the clutch by pushing the holding (catching) hand, bend the wrist backward with a passive hyperextension, flex the supporting hand, and lift the holding wrist upward.

5. Set the ball to shoot or pass by clutch-twisting the cups and holding the ball on the *FSC* of the shooting (catching) hand. This step sets a static triple threat (figure 9-C).

6. The cup is optimized in size by coordinating the arches and rays of the shooting hand: pressing the proximal transverse arch, extending the DTA and longitude arches, and abducting the four finger rays.
7. Push for shot or pass. Lift the ball with two hands, ensure the precise *4u1* of the shooting hand, and start to push for shot, pass, or a fake.

Releasing Process

Figure 10. Ball release for passing

1. The supporting hand leaves the ball for one-handed shot or pass.
2. The shooting hand lifts the ball farther with the shooting *FSC* (figure 10-A).
3. Start to shoot by flipping wrist on a jumping push initiated by the shooting-side stepping foot.
4. Thumb leaves the ball while *MAP* pushing the ball and index finger guiding it.
5. Extend *MAP*, pushing with slightly backward ball spin (figure 10-B).
6. Index finger leaves the ball while *MAP* shooting it.
7. Little finger leaves the ball while middle and ring fingers release it.
8. Middle finger leaves the ball before ring finger finally releases it.
9. Hand follows the shot by ring finger pointing to the target (figure 10-C).

One-Hand-Only Process

This is the process of one-hand ball control of *3fz* mechanism without the other hand's touching the ball. The process is for continuous dribbles, one-hand-only passes, and one-hand-only shootings.

1. After catching the ball, add index finger to the side surface of the ball to have more control.
2. Support the ball with thumb and form an *FSC* with a prehension grip and a radial deviation.
3. Carry the ball momentarily, in a dynamic triple threat, to intended position for changing directions in dribbling or passing, or lifting in shooting or passing.

4. Keep the *4u1* alignment in the whole process.
5. Change the directions of the ball movements in pass or dribble by turning the wrist in flexion or deviation of the DTA.
6. Lift the ball for shot or pass by extending bending wrist backward on *FSC*.
7. Shoot the ball out to the intended direction for shot, dribble, and pass in the exact same way as a shooting process.

The *3fz* mechanism with *4u1* alignment enables secure, smooth one-hand control of the basketball, whether to pass, shoot, hold, or fake the ball. Everything you do with two hands, you can do with one hand. The *3fz*'s *FSC* sucks the ball and gives the greatest scopes of basketball-holding movement. That leaves the other hand free to keep your balance and protect the ball in the holding hand.

3fz Dribbling

Dribbling by *3fz* is a creative process. It is a dynamic application of *3fz* techniques by coordinating the whole body in various dribbling skills with drives and moves. The paces, bounces, actions, fakes, and dynamic triple threat can be very creative and even artistic with *3fz* dribbling.

Tendons, Ligaments, and Muscles Build-Up

In dribbling, active involvements of *MAP* stimulate the hand's intrinsic and extrinsic muscles as well as ligaments and tendons. *FSC* formation and *4u1* calibration help build internal neural connections and muscle memories among the fingers. Dribbling the basketball actively involves all hand movements with their associated structures, mechanisms, and functionalities. Therefore, dribbling drills are not only for the acquisition of ball skills but also for a powerful hand with strong tendons, ligaments, muscles, and bones and articulations.

Drill 1. *Dribbling with fingertips*

Dribble the ball using only five fingertips (not pads) and try to stress the ring and little fingers. This is a good initial warm-up of the whole hand and a self-consciousness training of the tendons and muscles for their functions and involvements with coordinated bones and joints. The drill enhances the hand's neural touches, feelings, and blood circulations.

Figure 11. OK dribbling

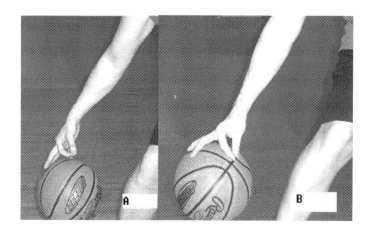

Drill 2. *MAP OK-sign dribbling (*figure 11-A*)*

Form an OK (okay) sign with both hands, with the straight index fingers touching the thumb tips. Extend *MAP* at the MP joints and slightly flex the IP joints. Start to dribble the ball in up-and-down motions, and use only the *MAP* fingertips to gently poke the surface of the ball. The purposes of this drill:

1. Establish the initial feelings of *MAP* touching the ball, focused at the ring finger
2. Stimulate the nerves and blood circulation among the *MAP* fingers
3. Build up the *MAP* muscles of PIs, DIs, and lumbricals, along with their associated mechanisms

This drill is a start of using *3fz* in dribbling basketball. Do it slowly and softly, taking a break if you feel any discomfort in the fingers. Do relaxation exercises outlined in chapter 6.

Drill 3. *OK dribbling with index finger* (figure 11-B)

- Continue OK dribbling by touching the ball to the ulnar side of index finger for more control.
- Do it just like five-finger dribbling.
- Handle the ball in slow motions by changing directions in small ranges.
- Alternate dribbling hands to actively rest *MAP*.
- Do simple and short dribbling drills in the beginning.
- Avoid any feelings of discomfort by taking frequent breaks.
- Progress to more complex and longer dribbling practices with stronger ring and little fingers.

The purposes of this drill:

1. Strengthen *MAP* to withstand passive forces of the basketball
2. Set up the new role of index finger in handling basketball with side touches
3. Establish internal signals of the acting bones, joints, palm, and wrist
4. Enhance the touches of the fingers and feelings of tendons and muscles

5. Distinguish the movements of flexion and extension, pronation and supination, ulnar and radial deviation, and finger abduction and adduction

Drill 4. *No-thumb dribbling*

This drill is practical in the game for simple one-side dribbles, in which there is no dynamic triple threat (hesitation dribble). Dribble the ball by *MAP* and straight index finger, with its ulnar side surface touching the basketball. Touch the ball first with *MAP*, and then add the index finger on the side surface to guide the ball but not push it. The purpose of the drill is to move the ball without the thumb for faster dribble transition, wider dribble scope, and more fingertip control.

FSC Formation

To fully control the basketball in *3fz* mechanism, it is necessary to form a Finger-Spring Cup in the dribbling hand. With *FSC*, a dynamic triple threat point can be established in every dribble. For *FSC* formation, you need to do the following:

1. Add the abducted thumb to the ball controlled by the four digits by touching it with the radial tip to the distal IP joint.
2. Do a wrist radial deviation with a prehension grip of five fingers and roll the ball to the top distal surface at the outer nail corner.
3. Actively flex the distal part of the thumb to press the ball against the opposed *MAP* to aim at a dribbling *4u1*.

This cup is able to suck the ball and hold it downward temporarily while changing directions.

The Dribbling 4u1

Universal Alignment is calibrated in *FSC* formation by adjusting the five finger rays and the DTA. In the process, the ball is rolling on the radial curve of the thumb tip to form dribbling *4u1* alignment.

In *3fz*'s *FSC*, there are four *4u1* alignments (figure 25) in slightly different ball positions on the thumb tip. In the upper middle section of the tip is the *4u1* alignment for passing and low-hand *UniShots*. The ulnar side of the thumb tip is the *4u1* alignment for up-hand *UniShots*. The other end of the alignments for passing, dribbling, and shooting is the radial tip of the ring finger, unchanged.

The detailed technical description of the *4u1* alignments can be found in chapter 7.

Five-Finger Dribbling

This is the regular *3fz* dribbling. First you cut and scoop the ball with *MAP*, and then you suck hold the ball momentarily in *FSC* for changing directions. At the end, you flip wrist and shoot the ball to the intended spot, controlled by the *4u1* alignment, and finally release the ball between the middle and ring fingers. The other hand actively receives the ball by its *MAP* and starts the same process.

After the dribbling *MAP* releases the ball with a shooting follow-through, the receiving hand's *MAP* catches the ball low as soon as it is bouncing off the floor. The process allows maximal ball-control distance and minimal time and distance for the ball flying free off the hand, therefore enabling secure, accurate, and dynamic dribbling.

In changing directions, your *FSC* sucking the ball allows the wrist deviations (ulnar or radial) and hand pronation as needed. In the process, *your index finger and thumb are always kept on top of the ball,* so it is not likely to be called palming.

Technical comparison of 3fz to the existing dribble techniques

- **Speed dribbling.** The *3fz* dribbles the ball with precise *4u1* in *FSC* with radian deviation and hand pronation, while the existing techniques dribblinig with proximate hand-arm coordination.
- **Crossover and cross legs.** The *3fz* dribbling uses *MAP* sweeping with radian deviation and supination instead of the commonly used forearm sweeping.
- **Inside-out dribbling.** The 3fz mechanism controls the ball by *FSC* with radian deviation, ulnar deviation, and hand pronation, while the conventional methods dribbling with finger, wrist and arm coordination.
- **Behind-the-back and spin dribbling.** The standard 3fz behind-the-back dribbling techniques are: *FSC* downward sucking, ulnar deviation, *FSC* hyperextension, the metacarpal transverse arch rolling, forearm swing, and hand supination. For this type of dribble, the existing techniques have no standard.

Pass and Catch

In *3fz* mechanism, passing the ball is just like shooting the ball. You catch and clutch the ball, and instead of shooting a *UniShot,* you shoot a pass out with one or two hands. In the passing process, *3fz* controls the ball in the same way as dribbling and shooting.

The *3fz* enables players to handle the basketball securely with a single hand. *FSC* locks the ball and can also roll, twist and spin it. The *4u1* alignment controls the ball's moving directions.

There are **three arms of force** (figure 4) in *3fz* one-hand ball-controlling mechanism.

1. The first one is **the power arm**, which is the distance from the wrist to the top of *MAP*. The shooting force generated by the whole body is applied to the power arm to produce maximal torque transferred by *MAP* to the ball. Ulna mobility and the DTA twist assist shooting torque generation along the power arm.

2. The second arm is **the power/control arm**, the arm of *4u1*, the distance from the thumb to the ring finger, generates static upright shooting torque and controls shooting direction, arc, and ball spin.

3. The other **control arm** is the distance between the index and little fingertips of *FSC*. This arm is used to change directions of the ball in pass and dribble, and to twist the ball for

sidespins in low-hand *UniShot*s under the basket. With the addition of index finger to *FSC* on the side of the ball, the hand can generate more twist torque in both pronation and supination moves.

One-Handed Pass

Like the one-handed shot, the one-handed pass has three stages: catching the ball, clutching the ball with two hands, and passing (or shooting) the ball with one hand to the intended position of a teammate.

The passes can be up-handed, underhanded, or side throws, and Universal Shooting Mechanism is always applicable, no matter how the passes are made. The *3fz* up-handed passes are technically similar to up-hand *UniShot*s such as high shot, scissors shot, or ear hook. The *3fz* underhanded passes follow low-hand *UniShot* techniques and have the variety of touch pass, reverse spin pass, half hook, side passes, and behind-the-back passes.

Two-Handed Pass

Passing with two hands is somewhat different. If the ball is right in the middle of your body, especially above your body, just easily adapt the regular chest passing or overhead passing techniques. If the ball is not in the midsection of your body, two-handed passing has the same process of two-hand *UniShot* shooting, with the same preparation and finish.

Comparison with the existing passing techniques

	Commonly Used	**3fz Passing**
Chest pass	Two-hand symmetric	Two-hand *RFT* by pushing *MAP*
Bounce pass	Two-hand symmetric or one-handed throw	One-handed or two-handed *3fz* shooting releases
Overhead pass	Two-hand symmetric	One-hand or two-hand *UniShot*s
Side pass	Nonstandard throws	Up-hand or low-hand *UniShot*s
Baseball pass	Underhanded throw	Low-hand *UniShot*
Behind-the-back	No standard	*3fz* behind-the-back dribble extended

Catch-and-Shoot

The *3fz* catch-and-shoot is the fastest move, with large variety and ranges. It makes it difficult for defense to challenge the shots. The vision, timing, and space created by *3fz* are much greater in the perimeters.

- **Catching hand is the shooting hand**. On catching the ball, the hand can start to shoot right away, no matter what direction the ball is coming from. The *3fz* allows you to adjust the body posture and balance to have a good open shot.

- **Pass to the far side of moving direction, away from defender**. If the ball is passed to meet your running, you can use your body and free hand to protect the catch (one-handed *3fz* catch). At the same time, you can turn your head or use peripheral vision to have a view of defense and the whole court. It is easy for you to decide whether to shoot or drive.

- **Make decision on ball catch**. Ball catching with *3fz* is a combination of dribble continuation, vision, and shot set. The instant or subconscious decision can be made in this split second.

Pass and Shot Fakes

Uniform posture of shooting and passing. After catching the ball, there is no difference in the posture or action for shooting or passing. You can shoot directly, make a fake, or opt to pass.

Unpredictable when mingled with moves and fakes. It is extremely hard for defense to predict the next *3fz* move after catching the ball. You can make the decision instantly and act right away; the defense has no time to react. If they gamble for one action, you will have easy options to drive, make a quick move to launch a step-away shot, or pass the ball to a teammate for a better shot.

Combination with variations and moves. The *3fz* allows more varieties for shooting, driving, passing, or faking. It protects the ball on the sides and has ambidextrous shots in wide ranges. The dribble is fast and low, while body posture stays upright in all the alternatives.

Chapter 3

UniShot: Universal Shooting Mechanism

UniShot, Universal Shooting Mechanism, is *3fz* implementation in shooting the basketball with the non-shooting hand assistance. It fundamentally distinguishes itself from the existing scoring methods in four technical aspects.

1. *UniShot* primarily uses **MAP**—Middle finger, Annular finger, and Pinky—to shoot the basketball, while the existing methods use the thumb, index finger, and middle finger.
2. *UniShot* shoots the ball in **Universal Alignment** and releases the ball off the ring finger, while the conventional method, standard two-handed over-the-head shooting, aligns the shots from between the index finger and middle finger to the shooting elbow and releases the ball off the index finger.
3. The *3fz* enables *UniShot* to control and shoot the ball with one hand and to produces **ambidextrous** shootings on a **one-footed or two-footed jump**. In contrast, the conventional method is strictly two-handed, two-footed shooting.
4. *UniShot* can be launched **up-handed** and **underhanded**, while the conventional shooting is up-handed, layup is underhanded, and other shooting throws like hook shots are mixed up-handed or underhanded shots.

UniShot possesses many practical features, such as shooting protection and side release, which the existing scoring methods do not have. The *3fz* one-hand ball-handling mechanism produces ambidextrous *UniShot*s in a large variety and with dynamic combinations, while the conventional shooting is uniformed and mechanical. Low-hand *UniShot* has significant advantages over the existing layups and hook shots in scoring range and accuracy, as does up-hand *UniShot* over the conventional shot. With overall technical edges, *UniShot*s have the capabilities to replace all the existing basket-making methods, including regular shots, hooks, layups, and various shooting throws.

Universal Shooting Mechanism includes its core *3fz* **mechanism**, **non-shooting hand assistance**, and **dynamic body-shooting alignments**. It inherits the fundamentals of basketball in physical conditioning, footwork, offensive stances, balancing control, moving with or without the ball, and dribble and pass combinations.

UniShot SHOOTING PROCESS

The Universal Shooting Mechanism produces a large variety of ambidextrous *UniShot*s in exactly the same shooting process: *MAP ball catch, FSC formation, RFT set, MAP shooting push,* and *ring-finger release*. The shooting process is the execution of Universal Shooting Mechanism dictated by its DNA *3fz* mechanism and *4u1* alignment. The non-shooting hand assistance contributes as an important factor of *UniShot*'s exceptional high accuracy and long range.

3fz Shooting Mechanism

The *3fz* shooting mechanism refers to **one-hand-only** shooting without the non-shooting hand assistance (no *RFT*). It has practical uses and advantages in certain game situations, but essentially, it is the core mechanism of *UniShot* for one-handed ball control in the whole shooting process.

The DNA of Universal Shooting Mechanism is *3fz*, the one-hand ball-handling mechanism, which primarily applies *MAP* to control the ball in the whole shooting process. The shooting power generated by the entire body is transferred through *MAP* and onto the basketball. In the process, the thumb supports the ball and adjusts **the shooting *4u1***, and the index finger is employed to guide the ball in the shooting release.

One-Hand-Only Ball Handling

Catching the basketball from dribble or pass, you always touch the ball first with the *MAP* fingertips on its outside (from body) surface. Then add the index finger, forming a sucking shovel, and scoop the ball up to meet thumb to form a Finger-Spring Cup (*FSC*). This cup, aligned to the ball's weight center from thumb to ring finger (*4u1*), controls the ball in different manipulating processes.

With *FSC*, you can manipulate the ball by prehension twisting, radial or ulnar deviations, or pronation or supination, carrying, lifting, or pushing it at your will. At the end, you shoot the ball to desired targets by flipping the wrist and releasing between the middle and ring fingers and finally off the ring finger. You can alternate your hands with the same procedure in dribbling, passing, and shooting.

The process of *3fz*, the standard one-hand ball-handling mechanism for dribbling, shooting, passing, and catching, can be simply described as a fluent procedure of the following:

1. Ring finger first touch
2. *MAP* ulna roll
3. *FSC* control in *4u1* alignment
4. *MAP* sweep or shoot
5. Ring finger release

Dynamic Finger-Spring Cup (FSC)

Finger-Spring Cup is **an imaginary cup without a brim** (figure 5), formed by the five digital rays of the hand. The formation of *FSC* is performed in the following way:

- Hold the ball with the *MAP* fingertips, the ulnar surface of the index finger, and the tip of thumb.
- Five fingers press the ball with the elastic forces of finger abduction and extension without contacting palm.
- As everyone has the ability to grab the ball using *3fz*, the firmness of *FSC* sucking the ball is dependent on the precision of *4u1* alignment.
- Bigger hands can use the fingers' pads holding the ball as long as hand's *4u1* is not compromised.
- Smaller hands can hold the ball down by touching the MP joints of *MAP*.

The purposes of forming *FSC* are to:

- Lock the ball with a single hand
- Shoot the ball with one hand in *4u1* alignment
- Dribble and pass the ball by finger and wrist manipulation

Four-Finger Cup

This is a *ball-sucking shovel* without thumb. The index finger is pressing with the ulnar surface on the ball caught by *MAP*. Four fingers are more spread out around the ball surface. This cup is useful in one-hand-only catches, high shots, underhanded shots, passes, and simple dribbling. More swing power and control range are generated in four-finger cup because of its far reaches in particular situations.

Universal Alignment (4u1)

In the *3fz* ball-handling process, maintaining precise *4u1* in hand is vital for secure dribble and accurate pass and shot. With its unique mechanics on the ball, *4u1* alignment ensures smooth ball handling. The alignment is like *the rifling of the 3fz gun*, which dictates the accuracy and precision of the shooting mechanism.

With precise 4u1 and a well-balanced body, you should not just make all attempted shots—but swish them every time!

Shooting Control

In the shooting process, *MAP* is always pressing behind the ball with their tips and pads. The three fingers are spread out on the ball, with bigger abduction between middle finger and ring finger. The ball may touch the protruded palm skins on the MP joints of *MAP* for the largest *FSC* size and ball-control area.

The index finger helps control the ball in guiding the shots, changing directions, or twisting sidespins. And thumb erects upright in a slightly abducted yet fully opposed position and supports the ball on the ulnar tip head near the upper nail corner. In this way, the palmar distal thumb is in precise *4u1* alignment with the radial sideline of the ring finger.

Dynamically structured by the five digital rays of hand, *FSC* locks the ball with great flexibility and stability in the whole shooting process. By adjusting the degree of thumb adduction without compromising *4u1*, we have variable sizes of *FSC* for different ball-control purposes.

Shooting Release

The ball is shot on *FSC* by the pushing force of *MAP* and released between the middle and ring fingers. But the ball finally leaves the hand off the tip of the ring finger, while the third lumbrical is actively in control. Real-time fingers' ball-releasing sequences are as follows: **thumb, index finger, little finger, middle finger,** and **lastly, ring finger**.

Kinesiology

With the slight flexed arm, *MAP* reaches the farthest (distances) to the body center (the hip) and the lowest (heights) to the floor. Two arms moving around the body form a dynamic umbrella to protect the basketball in dribbling actions, which can be flat and scoping with lower body stances. Ambidextrous hands (*FSCs*) alternatively control the ball in dribbling, passing, or shooting. By taking advantage of ulna mobility and radian stability, *4u1* alignment ensures fluent body coordination, resulting in smooth ball handling.

The *3fz* mechanism generates maximal shooting power and control since:

1. *MAP* is associated with the best body-shooting dynamics encompassing pushing, flipping, swinging, spinning and twisting, and so on.
2. *MAP* and thumb are structured in two major power and control arms of the hand (figure 4) to generate spring power (moment) by applied elastic forces of the body's joints and ligaments from foot to hand.
3. *FSC* enables stable control of the ball with its ball-holding structure for smooth application of the shooting power on *MAP*.

Universal Shooting Mechanism

UniShot—Universal Shooting Mechanism—is the combination of *3fz* (one-hand-only) shooting mechanism and the non-shooting hand assistance. By adding Reverse-Finger Twist (*RFT*) and clutch in the process, *UniShot* becomes powerful and potent in basketball shooting accuracy, range, and variety.

Two-Handed Shooting Set

The *3fz* one-hand-only shooting mechanism is the DNA of Universal Shooting Mechanism. In basketball games, it is necessary to hold the ball or set the shots with two hands for safe ball possession. However, innovative of *UniShot*, the primary objective of involving the non-shooting hand is to **protect** the whole shooting process, from ball catch to shot set and release. In the shot set, the non-shooting hand covers the front of the basketball against slap and steal.

Reverse-Finger Twist (*RFT*) on two-handed ball clutch, a natural human skill like opening a screwed jar, is a unique technique of *UniShot*. In the short process of *RFT* clutch, besides performing triple threat tasks and ball protection, it also sets or adjusts for precise *4u1* alignment. With two-handed shot set, *UniShot* can be launched with either one hand or two hands.

Reverse-Finger Twist (RFT) Clutch

Technically, *UniShot* is the integration of *3fz* one-hand-only shooting mechanism and *RFT* clutch. With *RFT* clutch, *UniShot* develops a variety of shots and drive combinations.

Figure 12. Reverse-Finger Twist

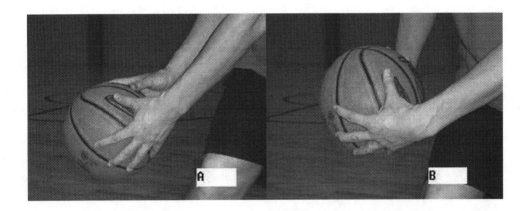

RFT clutch is a short, sudden, and powerful action; in the quick clutch, it performs three tasks: **protection, shot set,** and **alignment**. It is like an automobile clutch for a jump start.

1. When the shooting hand catches the ball on *FSC* and carries it up by flexing wrist and swinging forearm, the non-shooting hand actively clutches the ball opposing the shooting hand (figure 12-A).

2. Instantly both hands twist the ball with a *RFT*. The shooting hand rolls inward with a radial deviation and the non-shooting hand outward with an ulnar deviation (figure 12-B).

3. This action sets the ball tight in the shooting *FSC*, adjusts to precise shooting *4u1*, and optimizes finger-pressing spots on ball surface for maximal shooting power and control.

Ball Lifting

On clutching the ball with two hands, you close the shooting elbow by adducting the upper arm. At the same time, hold the ball up to the shooting-side shoulder, while the wrist is hyperextended to the backward position by pressing the non-shooting hand on the top of the basketball. Aiming at the rim with **peripheral vision**, you maintain a triple threat stance by keeping the upper body straight and the feet ready to step in to push for shot.

Peripheral Vision

UniShot uses peripheral visions of eyes to aim at the rim, while the conventional shooting method focuses the eyes to the basket by aiming at it. Not directly looking at the basket, *UniShot* has many shooting advantages:

- It is hard for defense to detect the shooting motion by looking at the shooter's head or eyes.
- A shooter's peripheral views can't be totally blocked. Shooters can always maintain good court vision including side views to the rim and onging defensive situations.
- Neurally, peripheral vision has extremely relaxed views, in which players react faster. In peripheral views, sprinters doing the one-hundred-meter dash have the fastest reactions at the starting signal.
- Peripheral vision for shooting is adjustable in the releasing stage by *3fz* mechanism, while the eyes are directly focused at the basket.
- It is deceptive with head and shoulder movements in dynamic triple threats.

UP-HAND AND LOW-HAND *UniShot*s

The *3fz* one-hand-only shooting mechanism allows players to shoot the basketball up-handed by pronating palm (down) and uplifting the arm, as well as underhanded by supinating palm (up) and low extending arm. It is effectively applied in Universal Shooting Mechanism for up-hand and low-hand *UniShot*s. Up-hand *UniShot*, either a one-handed or two-handed shot, looks like a regular shot, while the low-hand *UniShot* is more of a layup, hook shot, or half hook.

The body postures and shooting forms of the up-handed and underhanded shots are very different. Up-hand *UniShot*s are launched with the body moving upward, while low-hand *UniShot*s with the body forward. Both being ambidextrous, up-hand *UniShot*s have a larger variety of two-handed and one-handed shots on one-footed or two-footed jumps, while low-hand *UniShot*s are mainly contralateral one-handed, one-footed shots, except for free throws.

By applying the *3fz* shooting mechanism in different hand positions, up-hand and low-hand *UniShot*s have technical differences in the following aspects: shooting preparation, power generation, and shooting alignment.

- **Shooting Preparation.** Other than one-hand-only shots, both up-hand and low-hand *UniShot*s set a shot with the non-shooting hand assistance. However, the up-handed shots are set by *RFT* clutch, while the underhanded only *RFT*. And the underhanded *RFT* twisting angles are much smaller, the shooting wrist is not back extended, and the non-shooting hand stays at the side instead of on top of the ball.

- **Power Generation.** Shooting powers are generated from two distinctive systems for the up-handed and underhanded shots. Up-hand *UniShot* uses more stationary and explosive power, while the low-hand *UniShot* mainly uses dynamic power with more momentum. The up-handed shooting power is generated by jumping feet, extended shoulders and back, and pushing arm. In contrast, the underhanded shooting power is produced by running legs, swinging arm, and extended contralateral body.

- **Shooting *4u1*.** Universal Alignment is the key of *UniShot* shooting accuracies. Since the hand positions and *FSC* ball holdings of two shootings vary, there is respectively a slight adjustment in *4u1* alignment. For up-hand *UniShot*, the thumb supports the major ball weight on its ulnar distal part above the distal IP joint and is aligned with the ring finger along the radial sideline. In low-hand *UniShot*, where the ball weight is mainly on *MAP*, the thumb's mid tip holds the ball and aligns with the ring finger's radial sideline.

Figure 13. Standard one-hand two-foot jump *UniShot*

Shooting Procedure of Up-Hand UniShot

1. ***Ball catch****. MAP* catches the ball.
2. ***FSC formation.*** The shooting hand forms *FSC* by adding index finger and thumb.
3. The non-shooting-side foot steps up.
4. ***Ball clutch.*** The non-shooting hand actively meets the ball on the shooting side.
5. ***Reverse-Finger Twist.*** Two hands flip up the ball with a jerk reverse twist (figure 13-A).
6. ***Leaning elbow.*** The shooting upper arm adducts to the body.
7. ***Shot set.*** Two hands *RFT* clutch the ball close to the shooting-side shoulder in the most hyperextended wrist position.
8. The shooting-side foot steps in (figure 13-B).
9. ***Shooting push.*** Push shooting first with legs and keep the body upright.
10. Lift the ball high with two hands, and then the non-shooting hand leaves the ball.
11. ***Lock the ball****.* Lock the ball on *FSC* and push shooting with one hand.
12. ***Body extension.*** Extend the legs and ankles with outside calves to generate shooting power.
13. ***Jump push.*** Push on two feet, jumping when necessary.
14. ***Arm extension.*** Extend the shooting arm and flip the wrist upward.

15. ***4u1 shoot out.*** Spring out the ball at *4u1* alignment toward basket and release off ring finger (figure 13-C).

16. ***Regain body balance.*** Follow the shot for offensive rebound.

Shooting Procedure of Low-Hand UniShot

Figure 14. A low-hand *UniShot* layup

1. ***Ball catch.*** When driving to the basket or receiving a pass with the opposite foot on the floor, you catch the ball with *MAP* of the shooting hand with extended arm on the back side of the body, opposite the defense.

2. ***FSC formation.*** The shooting hand forms an *FSC* at the far side of the forward-swinging shooting-side leg. The non-shooting hand lifts up in the driving direction to protect the ball on *FSC*.

3. ***Shooting-side foot stepping up.*** Push powerfully with the opposite foot to make a big forward step on the heel of the shooting-side foot. The swinging non-shooting arm meets the ball on the forward-carrying shooting hand. The body stays straight and low and moves with speed and power to the basket (figure 14-A).

4. ***Reverse-Finger Twist.*** The non-shooting hand actively meets the ball low on the shooting side, while the body weight is on the shooting-side foot. Make an outward *RFT* (pointing outside rather than to the basket) right on clutching the ball with two hands, where the shooting hand is behind the ball and the non-shooting hand beside the ball. This action sets the ball tight on the *FSC* and ensures correct *4u1* alignment of the shooting hand. Then the shooting-side foot is ready to push for the opposite jumping step.

5. ***Ball holding and protection.*** According to defensive presences, two hands hold and protect the ball on the far side or rear side of the body. If there is one-side defense, the ball should be held to the far side, away from the defender. When it is a breakthrough situation, the ball should be held tight close to the body for better protection against possible steal.

6. ***Forward drive.*** Move the ball forward on *FSC* with the shooting elbow leaning the body. Contract the muscles of the shoulder, back, and arm and aim the ball at the rim by keeping the elbow aligned with the ring finger. Then the opposite foot makes a strong and quick shorter step on the heel to transfer the momentum to maximal jumping power (figure 14-B).

7. ***The non-shooting hand leaves the ball.*** When the opposite foot is ready to jump with explosive power and the ball reaches the front with flexibly extended shooting wrist and contracted body muscles, the non-shooting hand opens up and protects the layup. Then the shooting arm starts to extend for the final shooting push.

8. ***Shooting push.*** On a powerful jumping push of the opposite foot, the shooting forearm swings the ball forward and upward swiftly while keeping the arm and elbow straight and aligned with *4u1* of the shooting hand. Keep the body upright and the non-shooting hand open in protecting position, especially when the defender is trying to reach the ball (figure 14-C).

9. ***Up in the air.*** When jumping to the highest point, your body's muscles are extending to extreme position to produce maximal shooting power and control. The contralateral shooting body (the shooting arm, shoulders, back, the opposite leg and foot) extend in a straight line to the basket while the whole system is aligned with *4u1* of the shooting hand.

10. ***Ball release.*** Flip up the shooting wrist and roll the ball off between the middle and ring fingers. Extend *MAP* pointing to the target and let the ball leave on the flexion of the ring finger lumbrical. Do a bit more supination when necessary (figure 14-D).

11. **Follow through** with the shooting arm and the extended jumping leg.

12. Continue to run toward the basket for possible offensive rebound.

Shooting Accuracy and Precision

The *3fz* shooting mechanism obeys human ergonomics. It comprises natural abilities of human beings genetically inherited from the long history of practice in the most traditional activities. The best examples of these activities are javelin throwing, male ballet dancing, and piano playing. Their moves are graceful, dynamic, powerful, accurate, and most importantly, natural.

Combining all these attributes, *3fz* mechanism projects a natural, smooth, and well-coordinated throw in an optimal trajectory, and propels the basketball accurately into the basket. In the process, *3fz* integrates power and dynamics of javelin throw, balance and coordination of male ballet dancing, and finger dynamics and accuracy of piano playing.

UniShot produces excellent shooting accuracy with its unique technical features. Universal Alignment makes the shots not only accurate but precise; you should not just make accurate shots, but swish every shot. The *3fz* mechanism also enables *UniShot*s to be launched even in unbalanced body postures with good accuracy. *UniShot*'s *RFT*—Reverse-Finger Twist—ensures precise *4u1* alignment and optimal *FSC* size of the shooting hand.

Long shooting push is another major technical edge of *UniShot* over the conventional shooting method. Its shot pushing distance (from set to release) is about twice as long as that of conventional shooting. It allows longer shooting control and at the same time generates greater shooting power. A good analogy of an up-hand *UniShot* is the combined move of javelin throw and shot put, while the conventional shooting push is like a dart throw. The power and dynamics allow long shooting ranges of *UniShot*.

The *3fz* mechanism allows *UniShot* to maintain Universal Alignment in hand for its static and dynamic shootings. The *4u1* alignment can be spontaneously coordinated with body postures in different moves and shots for **dynamic body-shooting alignments**. In comparison to the elbow-in to index finger alignment of the existing shooting method, *UniShot*'s dynamic body-shooting alignments have significantly lower requirements of flexibility and physical conditions of players. They utilize more resources of the human body and generate greater shooting power and control, consequently producing higher shooting accuracy.

The technical advantages of *UniShot* over the conventional shooting method and detailed analyses are listed in chapter 8.

Dynamic Body-Shooting Alignments

UniShot's dynamic shooting alignments are all natural mechanisms of the human body. These alignments have been commonly applied in other sports such as volleyball, track and field, soccer, and more.

Figure 15. Body-shooting alignments

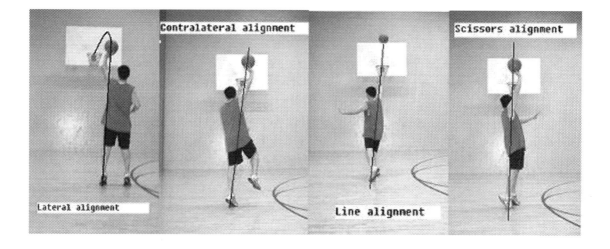

- **Shooting-Side Lateral Alignment** for two-foot up-hand *UniShot*s: the ring finger, forearm, triceps, shoulder, back, quadriceps, outer calf, and outer heel of the shooting side bodies, e.g., the right foot, leg and shoulder to right-handed shooting, or left-side bodies to left-handed shooting
- **Contralateral Alignment** for one-foot up-hand *UniShot*s: the shooting ring finger across the body to the opposite foot's outer heel, e.g., left foot to right-handed shooting, or right foot to left-handed shooting
- **Line Alignment** for underhanded *UniShot*s: the shooting ring finger along the jumping (one-footed or two-footed) line to the basket, e.g., the shooting hand, two jumping (or stepping) feet, and the basket in the same line
- **Scissors Alignment** for scissors *UniShot*s: the shooting ring finger, elbow, and triceps to back muscles and the outer heels of both feet in the same line

For all *UniShot*s, the shooter should keep her body's dynamic alignments in the same direction as the basket. In the shooting practice, their bodies' spring power should be first applied for the shooting alignments, and then muscle power added for more power and control.

UniShot body-shooting alignments can be dynamically and automatically adjusted by *3fz* conditioning. All you need is to focus on *MAP* ball catch, *FSC* formation with quality *4u1*, *RFT* set, and *3fz* shooting control. The key elements of dynamic *UniShot*s are court visions, balanced body, and great *3fz* skills.

Shooting Control

UniShot has long shooting pushes; they can start from knee high to the spring point—the highest ball-releasing point where only elastic power is applicable. In the long pushing distances, *3fz* mechanism generates more natural, dynamic shooting controls to the process. The shooting controls are contributed by dynamic balance, body extension, arm swing, wrist turn or flip, and finger rolls. By involving and coordinating most major muscle groups, *3fz* mechanism makes *UniShot* a smooth, relaxed, and dynamically powerful shooting process.

UniShot is also a quick shooting mechanism, as *3fz* gives it natural and fluent ball controls. The shooting speed and accuracy are entirely dependent on the shooters' *3fz* skills. The more efficient ball handling with *3fz*, the faster you can release shots—and the more accurate and precise the shots are.

Shooting Power

With Universal Shooting Mechanism, a player can produce as much shooting power as that of throwing a full crosscourt pass with great accuracy. They are actually the same action involving most muscle groups and coordination and dynamic body movements such as running, jumping, turning, swing, and pushing.

UniShot Shooting Mentality and Philosophy

- Keep good court vision and peripheral view to the basket.
- Maintain low body postures and keep good balance.
- Post strong static and dynamic triple threats.
- Make decisions according to defense.
- Dedicate to the teamwork and pass first mentality.
- First apply elastic power of the shooting bodies.
- Launch only clean shots.
- Protect the ball and the body all the time.
- Land in good balance by swinging the free arm.
- Always step in after every shot and get ready to rebound.

Chapter 4

Shooting Problems
with the Conventional Shooting Method

Different from other popular sports such as soccer and volleyball, basketball gives its participants an overall workout of their upper bodies as well as lower bodies, and it allows them to play with similar skill sets for all five positions.

Track and field events are the fundamental physical activities for all sports, which are composed of three essential athletic elements of running, jumping, and throwing. As a major professional sport, basketball involves all of those elements, while baseball has minimal jumping activity, ice hockey has little jumping and no throwing, and the linebackers of American football engage in limited running or jumping in their games.

In basketball games, players have free and creative movements of body, trunk, and limbs, especially of hands and arms, while soccer is played primarily with legs and feet. Basketball players, of all five positions, are trained with equal skill sets. In football, quarterbacks, linebackers, and wide receivers require totally different skill sets and training. In goalkeeping sports, goalies are in isolated positions from their teams in terms of skills and training.

With the moves, passes, tricks, and so many ways of scoring, basketball is a game full of spectacular plays. People enjoy playing or watching the game because they want to have the physical dynamics, mental excitement, and creativities of basketball.

However, the basketball shooting is a rigid part of the game. It lacks variety, dynamics, and creativity. The sole incentive of players for spending most of their training time in shooting practice is that the conventional shooting method is the most effective way of scoring three-pointers. That is the reason that the modern basketball produces so many dedicated, strong-willed shooters—because they can dramatically change the game results with their three-point shots.

CONTRAST OF SHOOTING ACCURACIES

A jump (or standing) shot is the prime scoring method in modern basketball games; therefore, it is the most practiced skill of the sport. In preparation of competitions, great shooters might make over 90 percent of jump shots in practice just a few hours before the game. But facing challenging defense, they can only score about 40 percent of their attempts during the game. That is the reality of professional basketball games. Clearly, the defensive pressure makes the huge drop (about 50 percent in the NBA games) in the shooting percentages.

The conventional two-hand over-the-head shooting, whether jumping or not jumping, is a hard and explosive shot. Long-range shots require great physical strengths. The shooting skill utilizes limited resources of the body, mainly the upper body. Ergonomically, the conventional shooting mechanics are rigid, unnatural, or too mechanical—not related to any common, traditional human civil or military activities such as lifting, throwing, pushing, swinging, turning, running, and even jumping (one-footed).

Learning the shooting techniques is a long, hard process, and it takes players years to practice. The training process is tedious and boring, and there is a lot of wear and tear and overuse in their body tissues. Professional players tend to gradually loss their shooting sharpness and range when they reach a certain age, around thirty-five years of age.

Biomechanically, the unnatural shooting mechanics are the main cause of declined shooting accuracies and early retirements of many professionals. It is disadvantageous to the majority of people (not big or strong) to play basketball by shooting that way. This method is not suitable for small children, women, and older players.

The following sections are the detailed technical analyses of the conventional shooting problems.

Alignment Problems

Ball Release between Index Finger and Middle Finger

In the conventional shooting method, the ring finger and little finger of the hand are not very useful. As a de facto shooting standard, the basketball is released between the middle and index fingers, though some experts recommend that the ball finally be tipped off the index finger. That way, the shooting power and control are concentrated on the first three fingers, the thumb, index finger, and middle finger, in the form of a "chuck" or tripod grip. The shot is set on a relatively small and unstable control area of the radian tripod on the ball, and the non-shooting hand support is needed. Therefore, for the conventional shooting method, one-handed shooting is technically feasible for practices and practically impossible in real games.

The ring finger and little finger of the shooting hand can support the ball in the shooting process, but they cannot, and should not, produce any power or control in the shooting push, since the two fingers are shorter than the middle finger and hold on the outside curvy surface of the basketball.

Because the ring finger and little finger are directly associated with ulna mobility, a turn (supination or pronation) of the palm will change the shooting direction or cause a sidespin on the ball. This is the reason that the two lower fingers should not be applied to generate any shooting power or control in the shooting process, except for temporarily supporting the ball for stability. In fact, even their support is unnecessary since there is the non-shooting hand support.

Elbow In, a False Shooting Alignment

Elbow in, to keep the shooting arm a straight line, is a desired alignment of the conventional shooting method. It requires good flexibility, which many players lack. Physiologically, it is unreasonable to form such an awkward arm position. Also, the elbow-in posture disobeys the basic principles of ergonomics for natural body movements and low impact of joints and muscles. It makes many players ignore the alignment; they just shoot the ball with the forms they are comfortable with.

Today's basketball players are used to shooting the ball with both hands, along the midsection of the body toward the basket. This shooting stance is commonly accepted for its game-situation practicality and effectiveness. You aim at the rim with your eyes, with the ball and the basket in the same line. In this stance, you can even shoot a double clutch or fadeaway without losing orientation to the target, and it is good to balance your body by jumping with squared feet.

The problem is that it forms an isosceles triangle, with your shoulder as the baseline and two arms as sidelines. When a player's flexibility does not permit a good elbow-in alignment, her shooting arm will be pushing the ball in the wrong direction, along one sideline of the triangle. Many shooters can adjust their shooting with their hands without good elbow-in alignment.

There are players who do possess the elbow-in flexibility that many young kids have. They have to align their arms to the shooting side of body in an odd stance, with their elbows sticking in the ribs for a skewed spine. This might yield a good shooting percentage with hard training, but that is extremely vulnerable to defense by shooting-side overplay. It is not useful in congested game situations, and there is rarely great outside shooters in that shooting stance, since it is contradictory to the inside shootings.

Therefore, elbow-in alignment is just a desired or proximate shooting posture for certain players. It should not be a standard for shooting alignment.

Squared Feet for Balance

Shooters must square their feet to balance their bodies, and it is the only correct footwork to keep good shooting posture. No matter what kind of move you are making—whether running, jumping, or turning—you must step or jump to square your feet in order to launch a makeable shot. That is the best way, and the only way, to keep the body balanced for good shooting posture; otherwise, the shooting accuracy would be extremely compromised. That also makes the conventional shots predictable for their uniformed foot-square shooting stance, and it gives defenders the opportunity and time to interfere with the shots.

Shooting Push

In the conventional shooting mechanics, the ball is pushed by the thumb, index finger, and middle finger, with limited power and control. The shooting hand sets the ball on the thumb and the radial palm, the portion near the MP joints of index and middle fingers. These three fingers are directly associated with radian stability. The shooting power is transferred through the radian to the wrist and then to the thumb and inner palm in a relatively small control area. With the pads of the index and middle finger touching the ball, it is hard to apply the fingertips to push and control the ball. It is difficult for players with bigger hands to shoot this way since the ball is relatively too small in their hands, and more palms and less fingertips are involved in the shooting push.

Shooting Alignment Summary

The conventional shooting alignment can be summarized as squared feet, elbow in, the first three-finger control, and index finger and middle finger release. This alignment is mechanically designed and trained, not a naturally possessed mechanism of players. Many players do not have the flexibility required for the alignment.

Because of the infeasibility of applying the alignment, players are shooting the ball in different nonstandard postures. Good shooters with smooth strokes and coordinated body posture usually have good flexibility in better elbow-in alignments. Their shots might be accurate, but the arms' position is odd and vulnerable to defensive interference. Other players without such good flexibility have different styles of shooting. Their postures, especially the hand and arm position, vary quite extensively. Many players do not care about the alignment; they are just shooting the ball with feelings and hard training. With great shooting mentality, many players with bad elbow-in alignment become good shooters through assiduous shooting training.

Shooting training with elbow-in alignment is tedious and boring. You have to correct or compensate for every detail since the alignment is physiologically not coordinated with your shooting posture. Players are not playing with their natural abilities or talents, but training hard for unnatural shooting mechanics. That could lead to occupational hazards of overuse injuries.

This alignment is extremely hard for players with broad shoulders. A number of NBA centers are having the same problem in the shooting alignment, and they have to give up the shooting technique, only scoring by hook, layup, and dunk.

Free Throw Problems

With its rigid mechanics, the conventional shooting is neither a stable ball-propelling process nor a biomechanically sound shooting technique; at least it should not be a standard for free throws. From the free throw line, in the same mechanics, professional players shoot so differently insofar as their hand positions, arm movements, and body coordination. Most of them struggle with the technique and make less than 80 percent of their free throws from that close—about fifteen feet (five meters)—to the basket.

Uniformed Free Throw Shooting Technique

The conventional two-hand over-the-head shooting method has become the standard form of free throws worldwide in professional and amateur games. As we discussed above, this shooting form is not suitable for every player. It is hard for players with bad shooting mechanics to make free throws, especially when they are pressurized in tight game situations.

Field Basket versus Free Throw

With the same shooting mechanics, free throw shooting percentage is very much in correlation with that of jump shots, as it is the only way to shoot free throws. It is evident in all levels of competition: good jump shooters are usually good free throwers; poor jump shooters are poor free throwers. And the worst free throwers (around 50 percent shooting on the line) rarely make the jump shots in the game.

Shooting Arc and Ball Spin

It is optimal that the ball is released with a high arc of over forty-five degrees and a slight backspin. Along the high trajectory with backspin, the ball has the good air dynamics and best geometrical and mechanical chances to enter the basket.

Two-Hand Cut with Low Arc

With two hands shooting the ball overhead, shooters might easily apply radial deviation of the wrists to generate more shooting power and consequently cut the arc low and generate sidespin. It is typical with fadeaway and off-balance shots. High arc shots need more power and good shooting alignment. Many players can't keep the shooting alignment when they are jumping; therefore, they can't generate more shooting power either.

Sidespin

Even the shooters have great shooting techniques, but under defensive pressure, it is hard for them to have a relaxed and smooth shooting push. In the situation of quick release or double clutch, the non-shooting hand tends to help push the shot, and then it often generates strong sidespin. For average shooters with less shooting flexibility, sidespin on a shot is a common symptom in the game. Technically, it is difficult to control ball spin when shooting with radial tripod, even in a one-hand shooting practice.

Fadeaway Shots

Fadeaway of the conventional shooting is a tough shot that is usually taken as the last scoring option. It needs tremendous physical strength in shooting high arc, or the shooting accuracy will be compromised by low arc or sidespin. In the fadeaway shot, players tend to lose their shooting alignment. To compensate the setbacks, players tend to shoot fadeaways using the backboard.

Shooting Power and Control

Biomechanically, the conventional shooting method involves limited muscle groups and body dynamics, yielding less shooting power and momentum. The shooting alignment allows minimal finger involvement and short shooting push, and it lacks finger control and adjustment in a short push.

Short Shooting Push Distance

The conventional shooting is a hard, explosive shot. The shooting force is applied to the ball in the uplifting process of hand and forearm. The measurable shooting push distance is about the length of the shooter's forearm. It is very difficult for players to generate enough shooting power in such a short push for long-range shots.

Control with First Three Fingers

In the past, two-handed shooting used to be like a volleyball setting or a high-arc chest passing. It produced great accuracy and long shooting range among female players. It had the advantages of long shooting push and control by six fingers of the two hands (three plus three). The modern two-hand shooting method has evolved to a two-hand holding and one-hand shooting overhead shot. The ring finger and little finger still remain uninvolved in shooting push and control, merely supporting or doing nothing.

The conventional method controls the ball by the first three fingers holding it like a chuck grip, which forms a small area from the MP joints to the tips of the fingers. It is inflexible in control adjustment while setting the shot, since the three fingers are directly associated with the radian stability (or immobility). Ball setting is not stable since the control area formed by the three fingers and inner palm is relative small in comparison to the size of your whole hand. The three fingertips are not actively pressing or pushing the ball; otherwise it can result in side spins and loss of control, as the combined force of the three fingertips does not point at the geometrical center of the basketball.

It is almost impossible to control the ball in such an explosive short push. Everything in the process is just the shooter's mental willingness to make the shots as practiced.

Limited Shooting Power

The shooting powers generated in the conventional method are static and one-dimensional. They are straight pushing forces, of chest, shoulder and legs, with little arm of shooting force for moment. The muscles involved in shooting are concentrated in these areas. There is no dynamic power (momentum) generated from the body's movements of swinging, throwing, springing, turning, spinning, twisting, and so on.

Vulnerabilities to Defense

As we stated in the beginning of this chapter, defense makes a huge difference in a player's shooting percentages. The following are detailed analyses on vulnerabilities of conventional shooting.

Uniform Body Movement and Shooting Posture

The conventional shots are launched in the same shooting process and body posture. They have strictly the same procedure and body forms: squared feet, balanced body, upright back and head, eyes on target, shot set in the middle, and ball over the head aiming at the rim.

When the body is slightly unbalanced, feet not perfectly squared, back or head a bit tilted, or eyes not focused on the target, the shooting accuracy will be severely compromised. Good shooters are trained specifically for strict postures of each body part involved in the whole shooting process. When shooting, they are like well-built machines doing the same move with the same functionality.

In real games facing tough team defenses, this uniformed body posture allows the defense easy anticipation and interference of the shot. Pressing defense with frequent body contact makes it hard for shooters to maintain their shooting balance. Waving hands and blocked vision can cause shooters to lose their focus on target.

Standard Shooting Procedure

The conventional jump shots have a unified shooting procedure. The shooters need to

1) catch the ball to the front of the body or jump or step behind the ball;
2) lift the ball in the middle front to set the shot in triple threat stance;
3) push the shot and square the feet; and
4) jump in the air and release the shot.

The defenders can execute their conventional approaches to this standard shooting procedure. In each shooting step, they just need to

1) try to steal the ball or poke it away, since the ball is not protected by shooter's body or arms;
2) use one hand to cover the shooting direction and the other hand to slap the ball;
3) put one hand in the shooter's face to block the shooting vision; and
4) jump up after the shooter and try to alter the shot.

The last step is the best time for a helping defender to block the shot.

Against the regular shooting routine, the defense has so many chances to steal or slap the ball, and block or interfere with the shot. Defenders can subconsciously anticipate shooters' standard actions and uniformed posture with their good footwork. This is why most shot blocks are by the weak-side defensive helpers. It consolidates the coaches' shooting philosophy of trying to get open shots all the time.

Hand Involvement

Two-Handed Shot

The conventional method uses two hands in the whole shooting process, from catch to set to release. With the small control area of a chuck grip by the first three fingers, it is very unstable to set a shot and almost impossible to shoot the ball with just one hand. Therefore, the non-shooting hand must support the shooting hand; the only advantage of the two-handed shot set is easy to change to a two-handed overhead pass.

Ambidexterity is not necessary because the shooting position is right in the middle, and you automatically use the dominant hand all the time for better shooting percentage.

Finger Involvement

The conventional shooting method is using primarily the first three fingers to shoot or control the ball. The fingers touch the ball on the pads where the fingertips are not actively controlling it. Ring finger and little finger are virtually not involved in the shooting process except for some insignificant side support. In other words, if the method is not necessarily including the two fingers, it leaves the resources associated with them unused.

Ball Control Mechanics

The conventional shooting is a hard shot with short shooting push and control distance. Shooting push usually starts from above the head to the releasing point of the extended forearm. In the shot set, the ball is controlled on the small area of three fingers' chuck grip. It lacks of finger involvements for controlling the trajectory of the ball toward the basket.

Hand Movements

The hands are moving mechanically in the process. For the major shooting force was directly transferred from the forearm to the wrist and the first three fingers through the stable radian bone and associated palm muscles, there is little dynamic power since the mobile ulna and associated ring and little fingers are not involved. Wrist-flipping power is limited, as only the radial carpal is involved.

Shooting Practice

Basketball shooting practices are time consuming, rigid, and physically tiring. It is an occupational hazard for professional basketball players since they have to do all the shooting drills on the single shooting hand. They have to shoot hundreds and thousands of times for their free throws, three-pointers, corner shots, forty-five-degree shots, bank shots, and so on every day. It is such a tedious long-term process. Good shooters are the most assiduous workers on the conventional shooting techniques, and mentally they absolutely have to believe in themselves and their shooting abilities.

One-Hand Practice versus Two-Hand Shooting

One-handed shooting practice is a static, imaginary shooting process to adjust the elbow-in alignment, high arc, and good ball spin. It is hard to adapt the practiced one-hand shooting skill to the two-handed shots in real games. This is why so many players always have low-arc and sidespin problems in their shootings. Their one-hand shooting practices do not help solve the shooting problems. When the alignment cannot be achieved, one-hand shooting practice has little meaning in improving the shooting skills.

Free Throw versus Jump Shot

It is obvious that players with bad jump shooting techniques will shoot low percentages of free throws. The problem lies in that they have to use their bad techniques at the free throw line; oftentimes, they were intentionally fouled by the defense in order to send them to shoot free throws.

Other than the conventional shooting method, no other mechanisms seem to be available for the free throw. And the method is incapable of helping free throwers. Ironically, these poor free throwers have to play hard near the basket and get fouled to shoot free throws. They have no other alternatives but to try their awkward shooting and score only half of their hard-earned opportunities. A problem comes out with a strange symptom in professional games called "Hack-a-Shaq." The existing shooting techniques have no solution for the ugly play.

Layup, Hook, and Floater

Layups, hook shots, and floaters have completely different techniques from the conventional shots. Therefore, they must be trained separately. Big players probably practice more for hook shots, and smaller players more layups. Hook shots, layups, and floaters have no technical standards; everybody uses freestyle. Besides the regular shooting practices, they have to spend time training all these different shots separately.

Dribbling Combination

In real game situations, shots with dribbling and driving make for a practical, dynamic, and powerful scoring combination. On the contrary, the conventional shooting method has very limited dynamics and shooting variety to dribbles and drives. Thus the existing dribble, drive, and shoot combinations are predictable and vulnerable to pressing defenses and weak side blockers.

Predictable

The regular shot on dribble is to the advantages of defense. First, it is not hard to anticipate the moves and shot. Second, when the dribble is used, the defender can start to play body-close defense, and then it is the best chance to double-team the dribbler. Third, no matter how dynamic your dribbles are, you end up shooting with the dominant hand, and the defender can simply overplay you on the shooting side. Even for great shooters, it is a major vulnerability that they can be overplayed on the shooting side. The defending team can also trap the shooters to force them in the direction in which they are uncomfortable shooting.

Time Consuming

The process of shot on dribble has three separate stages:

1) Catch the ball on dribble with two hands and swing to the middle line of the body.
2) Lift the ball to shoot and jump up on the squared feet.
3) Hang in the air, contract the shooting muscles, and push the shot.

There are two short stops between the three stages. The purpose of the two stops is for the muscle contractions of lower and upper bodies. They generate the jumping and shooting power and also consume more time. It gives the defense the opportunity to react, move, and interfere with the shots. These are the major causes of the big drops in shooting percentages between the game situations and shooting practices.

Lack of Variety

The conventional shooting on dribble is uniformed. Every time you catch the dribble, you need to swing the ball to the middle, square the feet, lift the ball up in the middle, jump, and stop in the air, and shoot. It is only way to practice and to shoot in the game for long-range shots. The defenses coming from any direction automatically know where and when the shot is launched. The simplest thing for them to do is lift their hands and move to that spot to challenge.

Catch-and-Shoot

Conventional shooting is a rigid mechanical process. The shooter must jump behind the ball, face the basket, square the feet, and shoot a one-directional jump shot. The whole team must coordinate their offensive action to produce this kind of open shot.

Chapter 5

UniShot Shooting Solutions

The discovery of Universal Shooting Mechanism with its *3fz* DNA reveals the disadvantages and technical inabilities of conventional shooting methods. *UniShot* has six basic shooting forms that provide comprehensive solutions to the shooting problems and challenges in modern basketball, about which we discussed in the last chapter. With significant technical edges, *UniShot*s have the capacity to overtake existing scoring methods completely.

The six basic *UniShot* forms are two-hand standard, one-hand standard, scissors, high-spring, back-extension, and low-hand *UniShot*s. All six *UniShot* forms can be applied for free throws and field goals. They are set in different shooting postures and dynamic body-shooting alignments, involve different muscle groups, and have their specialties and advantages for different game situations.

Shooting Mechanisms and Techniques

The core element of *3fz* mechanism is Universal Alignment, which can be acquired by systematic conditioning and training of hand and fingers as a permanent skill. Each time you catch the basketball, your hand should instantly adjust to *4u1* alignment on the ball surface to its geometric center. Whether you are shooting, dribbling, or passing, it should be a subconscious action.

As you set to shoot the ball, your wrist, elbow, arm, shoulder, back, waist, legs, knees, and feet are automatically aligned with the shooting *4u1*. In other words, your shooting body from arm(s) to foot (feet), the hand's *4u1*, the basketball, and the basket are kept in a straight line in every *UniShot* form. In the same principle, *UniShot* has four dynamic body alignments for different shooting forms.

Basketball players have different sizes, body structures, athletic talents, skill levels, and genders. Although the six *UniShot* forms offer shooting variety suitable for each individual, you should command all six for complete shooting skills. After you first command *4u1* alignment and *3fz* mechanism, you should not have any problem in shooting *UniShot* of any form. However, you might favor one over others in shooting free throws, or choose one that yields better field goal percentage.

The objectives of *UniShot*'s six basic shooting forms are to provide practical shooting techniques adaptable to players with different physiques by exploring their natural talents in shooting the basketball. Each form is technically related to practical scoring in specific game situations. The six *UniShot* forms will help the players who are unable to convert the conventional shooting techniques and bring them technical solutions to become good shooters.

Free Throw versus Field Goal

Free throws are the technical standard of field goal shooting. They are typical midrange standing shots. Professional players are using the conventional method as their basic shooting form, and it is so far the sole standard of free throw shooting. The majority of the professionals shoot field goals in the same way, either standing or jumping, in making mid-range or long-range baskets, as they do for free throws. There is a strong correlation between the shooting percentages of free throws and field goals.

TWO-HAND STANDARD *UniShot*

Two-hand standard *UniShot* adopts the body posture, footwork, and shooting preparation of the conventional shooting, except for hand and arm involvements. Technically, two-hand *UniShot* is distinguished from the conventional two-hand shot by its core mechanism *3fz* and the shooting *4u1* alignment. It is the standard of all up-hand *UniShot*s.

Shooting Form

Figure 16. Two-hand and one-hand standard *UniShot*s

Posture and Stance (figure 16-A and B)

The body posture and stance of two-hand *UniShot* are almost identical to those of conventional shooting. After catching the ball, you need to square both feet and set the shot in triple threat stance by lifting the ball aiming at the rim. Finally, you extend your body and shoot the ball in the same posture of a conventional shot.

Shooting Process

Having the conventional body posture, two-hand *UniShot* brings many technical improvements. It controls the ball with *3fz*, sets the shot by *RFT* clutch, aligns the body on the shooting side, pushes shooting by *MAP*, and finally releases the ball off the ring finger.

Ambidexterity

With *3fz* training, two-hand standard *UniShot* can be spontaneously ambidextrous by catching and shooting with the same hand. Left-handed and right-handed shots should yield the same shooting accuracy, as they are symmetrically trained in *3fz* conditioning.

Shooting Release

The two-hand *UniShot* releases the ball between the ring and middle fingers and finally off the ring finger. The release is controlled by shooting *4u1* and the vertical shooting-side body alignment from the outer heel to knee, shoulder, elbow, and wrist.

Shooting Sequence

1. Catch the ball with the shooting hand.
2. Step up with non-shooting side foot.
3. Two hands clutch the ball with *RFT*.
4. Turn body to the basket and step in with the shooting-side foot.
5. Set the shot by lifting the ball to a triple threat stance. This move consists of hyperextending the wrist, pressing of the non-shooting wrist, up-pushing the forearm, leaning of the elbow, and aiming at the target (figure 16-A).
6. Lift the ball by two hands with straight back.
7. Raise the outer calves and heels to jump, stressing the shooting side.
8. On the jump power, flip up the wrist to shoot the ball on *FSC* (figure 16-B).
9. Release the ball between the middle and index fingers and finally off the ring finger.
10. Extend the body, control the landing balance, and then follow the shot.

Shooting Techniques

Ball Catch

1. Extend the shooting arm and hand with slightly flexed elbow and *MAP* to catch the ball from a pass or a dribble. The *MAP*-ball meeting point should be as low as possible to the floor. For low-catch positions, the knees should be deeply bended and the upper body kept straight.
2. First you touch the ball by the *MAP* fingertips, poking its outside surface, and extend *MAP* passively back by the bouncing ball. Flex the wrist and roll the ball up to *MAP*'s MP joints. Then extend the elbow and wrist to push the hyperextended MP joints with the ball outward.

3. Sweep the ball by the outstretched *MAP* with a combination move of active *MAP* flexion and slight palm supination, and scoop it up with a radial deviation of the wrist. Turn the ball inward with the guiding index finger to meet the supporting thumb to form an *FSC*.

RFT Clutch

1. The non-shooting hand moves actively to the ball in the shooting hand.
2. The hand touches the ball first with *MAP* and then clutches it by swing power with the shooting hand. Two hands (*FSCs*) spread fingers on the opposite surfaces of the ball like automobile clutch paws (springs) pressing on the discs. Then press the ball to the shooting hand for firm possession and protection.
3. Instantly two hands twist the ball in reverse directions (*RFT)*, with the shooting wrist turning inward (radial deviation) and the non-shooting wrist outward (ulnar deviation). The ball is held and twisted on the fingertips of the shooting hand, while the non-shooting hand adjusts the ball position and sets it in precise *4u1* alignment of the shooting hand.
4. Close up the shooting elbow to the shooting side of the body and lift the other elbow in front of chest.

FSC Settings

1. The shooting hand pushes the ball up with the hyperextended wrist by leaning the shooting elbow to the body and the non-shooting hand pressing on the top.
2. Instantly, the shooting hand forms a tight *FSC*, with the adducted and fully opposed thumb and the abducted *MAP*, to hold the ball and aligns *4u1* to the rim.
3. The shooting-side foot steps in low, with the erected back in a triple threat stance. Lock the ball on *FSC* close to the shooting side of the chest.

Shot Set

1. Two hands lift up the ball on the shooting *FSC*.
2. The non-shooting hand presses the ball to the MP joints of *MAP*.
3. The shooting wrist extends backward under the ball and bends passively to maximal angle.
4. Hold the ball close to the shooting-side shoulder and aim at the rim using peripheral vision.
5. Keep the body low by flexing both knees.
6. Extend the back up and step in with the shooting-side foot. In this triple threat stance, you are ready to push the shot.

Shoot and Release

1. Lift the ball farther up to push shooting.
2. The shooting-side foot pushes to jump.
3. Slide the non-shooting hand to lower ball surface.
4. Push to shoot the ball with two hands.
5. Flip the shooting wrist on the jump power.

6. Keep *4u1* alignment and release the ball between the middle and ring fingers and finally off the ring finger.
7. Follow through the shot with fully extended arm.
8. Land in balance by adjusting arms and body, then step up and get ready to rebound.

Practical Game Uses

The two-hand *UniShot* is the basic form and standard of other up-hand *UniShot*s. It is effective in congested game environments, where there is no space for a one-handed release. The shots can be opted to quick releases or floaters on a one-footed or two-footed jump. Here are just a few practical shooting situations.

- **Combination with fake and pass.** The advantage of two-handed shots is that the ball can be held back by both hands to opt to pass or dribble, just like the conventional two-handed shots.

- **Shooting in congestion.** In congested game situations, such as close to or underneath the basket, or with limited space, two-hand *UniShot* saves time and space, also protecting the ball.

- **Quick releases.** Two-handed quick releases are efficient for running floaters and under-basket quick shots. Low two-handed chest releases with the back against the defender are effective near the basket.

- **Pick-and-roll situations.** *UniShot* ambidexterity enables the dribblers to use the pick-and-throw quick shots with either hand, in both strong and weak sides.

- **Double clutch.** Just like the conventional shots, it can be used in congested or blocked situations. Double-clutch shots are good in drawing fouls and changing decisions.

- **Low release, hidden shot.** When under the basket with your back against a defender, you can release *UniShot* low at the waist while your body functions as a shield of the shot.

- **Runners.** Two-handed shots can be made with good shooting controls on one jumping foot or with off-balanced body.

- **Floaters.** One-footed or two-footed floaters are highly effective with two-handed releases.

- **Sneakers.** When one-hand *UniShot*s in congested situations are not possible to launch, you can opt for a sneaking two-handed shot around the defender.

- **Three-pointers.** Two-handed three-pointers are good timing in high-pick situations with quick releases.

ONE-HAND STANDARD *UniShot* (figure 16-C)

This is the standard for one-hand up-hand *UniShot*s. It is based on the two-hand *UniShot* in shooting forms and techniques. Only the last shooting push stage is controlled by one hand. Since *3fz* enables one-handed basketball control, the non-shooting hand just has the assisting role in shot set and ball protection.

The one-hand *UniShot* has advantages over the two-handed shot in involving more body and muscles for more shooting power and control. The one-hand *UniShot* allows players to use dynamic body alignments and peripheral vision to shoot the ball without facing the basket. With ambidextrous capabilities, the *3fz* mechanism gives *UniShot* shooting dynamics and variety.

Shooting Form

One-hand *UniShot* settings take the basic form of two-hand *UniShot*. Preparations are exact the same before the non-shooting hand leaves the ball. Only the last shooting stage is different.

Body Weight on the Shooting-Side Foot

For the one-hand *UniShot*, the body weight can be dynamically moved, not necessarily in the central line of the body. When the body is moving, your feet move coordinately to keep good balance. The one-hand *UniShot* can be launched on one foot, two feet squared, or two feet scissors.

Shoot and Release Stage

1. Keep the shooting-side alignment from heel to knee, shoulder, elbow, and to the hand's *4u1*.
2. Raise outer calves of both legs by stressing the shooting side and get ready to jump.
3. Two hands lock the ball high on the shooting *FSC*.
4. The non-shooting hand opens up to protect the shot.
5. One-hand shooting push in straight line on the jump power.
6. Extend the shooting shoulder for longer pushing and control distance.
7. Release between the middle and ring fingers and finally off the ring finger.
8. Follow the shot with balanced body to rebound.

Shooting Techniques

MAP ball catch, *FSC* formation, two-hand *RFT* clutch, and lift and set are standard techniques of two-hand *UniShot*. The following are the technical specialties of the one-hand *UniShot* shooting release.

1. Set the weight on the shooting side.
2. Balance the body by stressing the side alignment.
3. Squaring the foot is not necessary since the body is not directly facing the basket.
4. Use the peripheral vision for one-handed shot.
5. Twist waist, swing arm, erect back, and extend shoulder to generate more shooting power and control.

6. The non-shooting hand can protect the shooting or help control balance for rebound after the release.

Practical Game Uses

- **One-footed or two-footed shots.** One-hand *UniShot*s can be launched on either one foot or two feet. With its ambidexterity, one-hand *UniShot* produces a large variety of moves and shots. You can shoot near the basket or use bank shots and make zero-angle baseline shots and middle-range and long shots.

- **Long-range shots.** One-footed or two-footed one-hand *UniShot* is accurate in long-range shootings. Three-pointers can be launched statically or dynamically. The shooting positions are far away from the basket anywhere in the offense half court. One-foot jump shot allows you to launch minus-angled (behind the basket) baseline three-pointers.

- **One-footed or two-footed jumpers.** Two-footed jumper can be used with triple threat combination, leaving you a clear path for offensive rebounding when challenged. The one-foot jumper is launched when the defender is closely pressing you, with a quick one-leg jump-away for a hard-to-challenge one-hand *UniShot*.

- **Runners and floaters**. Running shots have a variety of high-runner, catch-and-shoot, jump-in three-pointers and step-out three-pointers. They are usually one-footed and efficient in team settings. Floaters are quick releases of one-hand *UniShot* runners.

- **Dribble combinations.** It is fluent to combine the one-hand *UniShot* with different dribbles and moves. Since every *3fz* dribble is a triple threat, one-hand *UniShot* on dribble can dominant defense with its shooting variety and moves.

- **Catch-and-shoot.** The *3fz* makes catching the ball so efficient, and one-hand *UniShot* catch-and-shoot is quick, triple threatening, and rhythmical. It can be one-footed for quick releases or two-footed for triple threat moves.

- **High pick 'n pop**. By using a high pick to three-point zones, you can create more opportunities to launch pick-and-shoot three-pointers. For ambidextrous *UniShot*, it is difficult for the defensive team to help on changeable pick/shot sides.

SCISSORS *UniShot*

Scissors *UniShot* has a concept of shooting the basketball with back to the basket, just like centers posting up in the paint. However, the scissors shot gives players of any size the ability to post up in the perimeters, far into the three-point ranges. Scissors *UniShot*s are two-footed shots with scissors-like jumps or steps.

Figure 17. Scissors shot

Shooting Form

1. Stay with the back to the basket and one leg leaning to your defender.
2. Maintain good vision of the court and keep peripheral view of the basket.
3. Hold the ball at rear, possibly far away from the defender.
4. Use your body as a shield for ball protection.
5. Keep the body low by erecting the back and turn the head around and look up for a triple threat fake.
6. Catch the ball with *MAP* in triple threat dribble (figure 17-A).
7. To take a shot, make a fake little spin-move with a drop step to the other side and show the ball to the defender.
8. Swing the body and ball by turning back and catch the ball up with *FSC* of the shooting hand.
9. The non-shooting hand clutches the ball at the body rear.
10. Set the ball with weight on rear foot by extending the shooting wrist backward with the supporting hand pressing on top of the ball (figure 17-B).
11. The front scissor foot steps forward, leaning to the defender.
12. Turn the straight body by twisting the waist and shoulder.
13. Lift the ball up with both hands while the back scissor foot is ready to step in.
14. Turn head to have a clean view of the basket and the court.
15. After ensuring the defense's position, lift the ball farther by *FSC* with one hand.
16. The other hand leaves the ball in a protective fashion (figure 17-C).
17. Jump on the toe of the rear scissor foot.
18. Push with the rear leg, swirl the shoulders up, and extend the elbow out.
19. The non-shooting hand opens up in a non-offensive angle to fence off possible defense interference.
20. Shoot push the ball by shoulder and forearm.
21. Flip the wrist and then shoot the ball on jumping power of the rear foot.
22. Release the ball on the ring finger (figure 17-D).
23. Extend body in a straight line.

24. Follow through with toe tip and the shooting hand.
25. Regain balance and get ready to rebound.

Shooting Techniques

1. A spin move is like a dribble with a drop step to fake or a fake step without dribble.
2. *MAP* catches the ball after a fake step to the opposite side, with head and shoulder involved in the fake.
3. Swing the ball swiftly to the shooting side by pushing the drop step foot.
4. The non-shooting hand clutches the ball with *RFT*, with the shooting hand under the ball, like shooting the ball to the opposite basket.
5. Lift the ball up with two hands by turning the shoulder and neck to have the rim in sight. Setting is the same technique of the one-hand standard shot.
6. Ensuring the absence of defense, start to push the shot by lifting the ball with both hands.
7. Step big to the opposite side foot forward with a scissors cut to the shooting side.
8. Quickly step a small chip step with the toe of the shooting-side foot to the back side of the body.
9. Shoot the ball by lifting with one hand and swinging it on *FSC* with the shooting arm, while the supporting hand leaves the ball and lifts up for shooting protection.
10. Turn the shoulder and back, flex both knees, and then raise both calves and turn the ankles by pointing the toes to the front basket.
11. Align the shooting hand's *4u1* to elbow and to the rear foot's outer heel in the same shooting curve to the target. This is the scissors body alignment.
12. Jump up by extending both knees and ankles and flipping the shooting wrist.
13. Release the ball between the middle and ring fingers and finally off the ring finger.
14. Extend the arm to follow through toward the target.
15. Regain balance after landing and get ready for offensive rebound.

Practical Game Uses

- **Low and high posts**. Big players usually stay in the low posts to play one-on-one, or to draw double-team and kick out to open teammates for open shots. Now smaller players can post up scissors *UniShot* in the perimeters to shoot long-range shots and three-pointers. The purpose of this high-post play is to draw defensive double-team in the perimeters and then make a pass to inside or outside open teammates.

- **Leaning shots**. Scissors shots are very powerful against pressing defense. You land on two feet after catching a pass in high post positions, and you can use a fake and turn to shoot with either hand against heavy body contacts of defense.

- **Baseline fake shots**. Near the baseline with the back to the basket, you can make a fake drive to the baseline and turn out to shoot a scissors jumper. When you are pressed to the corner by a double-team, you can also make a fake drive to the sideline and turn to the baseline corner to launch a corner scissors three-pointer. It is almost impossible for defense to challenge the head leaning scissors jump *UniShot*.

HIGH-SPRING *UniShot*

The high-spring shot is powerful for its high shooting positions. High *UniShot* is a typical *3fz* one-hand-only shooting mechanism with occasional non-shooting hand support; it allows players to have good vision, ball protection, and high-dynamic positions for shot and pass. High-spring *UniShot* shoots the ball with maximal body extension at spring point, which is the highest shot set, with only elastic forces of joints and ligaments applicable.

Figure 18. High-spring shot

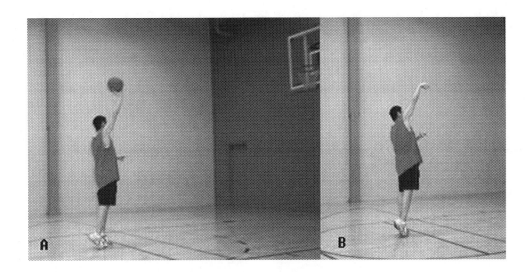

Shooting Form

1. Set the ball over the head with two hands ready for a pass or fake.
2. Ensure that your defender stays low and have a clean vision of the court.
3. Protect the ball with fakes and rear-foot steps and use front foot as pivot.
4. Set the ball high with the shooting hand *FSC* to spring point (figure 18-A).
5. Keep body straight and lean toward the defender.
6. The rear foot steps in and ready to push the shot.
7. Jump up on the spring powers by pushing calves.
8. Flip wrist and up dump the ball on *FSC* with shooting *4u1* (figure 18-B).
9. Release the ball between the middle and ring fingers and finally off the ring finger.
10. Regain the balance after landing for rebound.

Shooting Techniques

1. Set the ball on *FSC* of the shooting hand and keep accurate *4u1* alignment.
2. One hand swings the ball high in faking, passing, and shooting actions.
3. Move the ball in spring power ranges, which are generated by elastic force ranges of the hand joints (CMs, MPs, and IPs), wrist, elbow, shoulder, waist, knee, and ankles.
4. Slightly flex the joints and move the shooting arm, in turning, twisting, waving, swinging, extending, or pushing.

5. Coordinate the joints for maximal spring power for shooting.
6. Use the other hand to support or protect the ball when necessary.
7. Shoot the ball with dynamic shaking joints and flipping wrist.
8. Use ankle jump, scissors jump, and toe push to push shooting the ball.

Practical Game Uses

The high-spring *UniShot* is a double threat in protective high position. The shot gives you good vision of the court and the basket for a clean shot or pass.

- **High riders.** When you drive to the basket or in the perimeters, you can simply lift the ball high with two hands or one hand and protect the ball for a high riding *UniShot*. It is powerful when you drive through two defenders by protecting the ball with two hands.

- **High lifts.** You can lift the ball high in either stationary or dynamic moves and make high one-foot or two-foot *UniShots*. The shots can be long ranged, toe-jumpers, high layups, or high scissors.

- **Fake and pass combinations**. When a smaller defender is closely guarding you, or a bigger defender staying low, you can stand up and lift the ball high with one or two hands to pass or shoot.

BACK-EXTENSION *UniShot*

Back-extension *UniShot* is a simple and isolated application of Universal Shooting Mechanism. It is easy to practice and practical to use. Back-extension shots are effective when the ball is at the far shooting side, coming from the opposite of your moving direction.

Figure 19. Back-extension shot

Shooting Form

1. Catch the ball from the far shooting side when the ball moves in.
2. Align the shooting-side shoulder and back with the shooting *MAP* facing the basket (figure 19-A).
3. Clutch the ball with the non-shooting hand to the shooting side.
4. Set the ball on *FSC* of the shooting hand with a passive wrist extension.
5. Elbow leans to the waist and hand mounts the ball to the shoulder.
6. Put weight on the front leg and flex both knees in low body position.
7. Align back, shoulder, and elbow to the shooting *4u1* to the basket and contract back muscles (figure 19-B).
8. Extend back muscles to lift the ball and get ready to shoot.
9. Lift up the calves to jump and shoot release the ball off the ring finger.
10. The shooting shoulder and arm follow through (figure 19-C).
11. Balance the body after jump to rebound.

Shooting Techniques

1. Catch the ball on the far side and drop a big step with the opposite foot backward.
2. Form an *FSC* by touching the ball with the MP joints of *MAP*.
3. The non-shooting hand clutches the ball and presses on the top to force the shooting wrist extending back to the shoulder.
4. Align back muscles to the elbow and the shooting hand *4u1*.
5. The shooting side foot step back to support the body weight.
6. Extend the shooting bodies: legs, shoulders, and arms, especially the back muscles to generate shooting power.
7. Direct the ball to the basket by middle and ring fingers.

Practical Game Uses

Back-extension *UniShot*s are effective in the game situations of catch-and-shoot or shots on dribble. It is a smooth shot when the ball coming behind you in the same moving direction.

- **Side-catch jumpers**. When the ball comes to the opposite side of your moving direction, you can catch it with the shooting hand and continue to move with a big drop step of rear foot and a short jump step of front foot to launch a back-extension jump *UniShot*. Even if you are not moving, you can make a big drop step for a side-catch jumper.

- **Quick releases**. Back-extension quick releases can be one-handed or two-handed and on one foot or two feet. They are quick and practical in transition games near the basket.

- **Sneakers.** In combination with high *UniShot* post up, you can alternate a back-extension sneaker. This shot can also be made when your body is off balance against defensive contacts for a plus-one play.

LOW-HAND *UniShot*

Low-hand *UniShot* is unique among *UniShot*s because of its low and dynamic release positions. It takes the exact shooting form of a conventional layup but applies *3fz* mechanism and *4u1* alignment for low one-handed shooting. With its dynamic shooting power and extended control, low-hand *UniShot* yields high accuracy in exceptional longer ranges than the existing layups.

There are varieties of other *UniShot*s derived from low-hand *UniShot* by alternating shooting arm positions, including side shot, ear hook, reverse layup, high-arc hook, and back-extension hook. These advanced *UniShot*s are not only technically feasible, with high shooting accuracies, but also practical and powerful in competitions. But first you need to command the basic techniques of underhanded shots and the core *3fz* mechanism.

Low-hand *UniShot*s can be launched either statically or dynamically. There are technically two shooting forms of the underhanded shots: moving form and standing form. The moving body shooting form of low-hand *UniShot* is shown in **figure 24**.

Moving Body Form

1. Catch the ball from a dribble with the shooting hand low at the rear side of the body, with the weight on the shooting-side foot.
2. Step forward big, with the opposite foot to the basket, by pushing off the shooting-side foot.
3. Lower your body by bending both knees.
4. Form an *FSC* on the shooting hand and push it horizontally, without killing the possibility of continuous dribbles.
5. Keep the straight body and good court visions, and align the opposite shoulder high to the basket.
6. The non-shooting hand and arm open slightly in front of the ball for protection; at this moment, you are in a dynamic triple threat while stepping firmly on the opposite foot.
7. Upon deciding the shot, make another big step and accelerate with the shooting-side foot.
8. The other hand clutches the ball with the shooting hand on the shooting side.
9. Move the ball horizontally forward, toward the basket, and make a low-hand *RFT*.
10. Keep the body straight and head up, maintaining good court views of help defense, open teammates, and the rim.
11. On setting an underhanded shot, assertively make a smaller but quick jump step with the opposite foot to transfer the horizontal momentum to maximal leaping speed. This action is done with a fast leg swinging and active heel stepping on the floor.
12. Two hands lift the ball up on the shooting side, with the shooting hand underneath the ball and the other at the side.
13. The shooting arm remains flexed, while the elbows bend to a near right angle, and leans to the waist.
14. The thumb points to the basket with low-hand *4u1* alignment of the shooting hand.
15. The shooting wrist extends passively back by the non-shooting hand pressing on the ball.
16. Jump up with the opposite foot by rolling the pad, swinging up the shooting-side leg, and erecting the body.

17. The supporting hand helps swing the ball up and leaves the ball with high-opened arm to protect the layup.
18. Swing the shooting arm by extending the shoulder to the target.
19. Extend the elbow to generate more pushing power.
20. Jump high with fully extended body and flexed up-swung shooting-side leg for most speed and power.
21. Flip the shooting wrist in *4u1* and release the ball between the middle and ring fingers and finally off the ring finger.
22. Follow through the shooting arc with the straight arm by *MAP* pointing at the rim.
23. Keep running to the basket after landing, for possible offensive rebound.

Figure 20. Low-hand *UniShot* for free throws

Free Throw Form

1. Make at least one dribble before the shot.
2. Dribble the ball at the rear side of body while the opposite foot steps to at least three feet behind the free throw line.
3. Catch the ball with *MAP* and hold it on *FSC* with a straight arm.
4. Shift the body forward on the stepping foot.
5. Clutch the ball with the non-shooting hand on the shooting side.
6. Slightly flex the shooting elbow and lean to the waist.
7. Extend the shooting wrist backward with the pressing non-shooting hand.
8. The shooting-side foot steps forward in front of the free throw line.
9. Two hands lift the ball to the direction of the rim while keeping the elbow aligned to the shooting *4u1* and pointing thumb to the rim.
10. Move the weight onto the flexed front foot with a straight upper body.
11. The non-shooting hand leaves the ball while two feet start to push the shot.

12. Extend the shooting arm while the shooting hand *FSC* aims at the basket (figure 20-A).
13. Push to shoot by raising calves and ankles and extending knees, the back, shoulder, and upright neck. The non-shooting hand swings back for balancing the shooting posture.
14. On pushing power, flip the shooting wrist to release the ball between the middle and ring fingers and finally on the ring finger.
15. Follow through with the straight arm and ring finger pointing up the trajectory of the ball to the basket (figure 20-B).

Shooting Techniques

1. When dribbling the ball, release with *3fz* and catch as low as you can.
2. Step the opposite foot strong to the open floor near the defender, with the shoulder and slightly opened arm as cushion, and move close enough to have contact with the defense but not to charge.
3. Suck the basketball with the formed *FSC* low at the back or side to protect the ball while making contact with the defender.
4. Adjust body balance by pushing the opposite foot and shifting the body weight low and fast to the open floor.
5. Stride big and low with the shooting-side leg and gain maximal speed.
6. The non-shooting hand clutches the ball with an ulnar deviation in *RFT* action. The shooting hand stays behind the ball with *MAP* back extended and abducted. The ball is moving on the fingertips by the pressing and twisting non-shooing hand for the adjustment of optimal size of *FSC* and precise *4u1* of the shooting hand.
7. Swing the opposite leg and foot and make a short and quick heel step to transfer the horizontal momentum to vertical speed.
8. Lift the ball up with two hands and make the final adjustment in *FSC* for relaxed body alignment from the shooting hand, elbow, shoulder, and back to the opposite leg and foot, and at the same time contract the body muscles ready for the shooting push.
9. Jump up with the opposite foot and shoot the ball with one hand.
10. Extend contralateral hand, arm, shoulder, back, and leg.
11. Shooting hand sticking out to follow through.

Practical Game Uses

Low-hand *UniShot* is the unique combination of *3fz* mechanism and regular layups. It produces accurate long-range layups in the three-point ranges. With its variety of different arm positions, it alone has the potential of replacing the existing scoring methods. Low-hand *UniShot*s can be launched at any distance and angle in the offensive half court. It has a great combination of dribbling, dynamic moves, and shooting protection.

- **Short-range layups**. You can use low-hand *UniShot*s for layups without using the board. It has high arc and is hard to block. Its quick releases on one foot or two feet edge out the existing floaters or any quick shots. You can also use the backboard for a high bank with finger rolls. It is superior to regular layups for pure *3fz* advantages.

- **Long-range layups.** They are unique shots since you can do layups from the free throw line and farther away from the basket. These are usually in jump shot ranges. You can also do three-point layups. They are not only accurate but also hard to block because of their high arcs, quick releases, and non-shooting hand protection.

- **Three-point fast breaks.** You can use long layups in four-on-three, three-on-two, two-on-one, or one-on-zero fast break situations. In the transition as a player initiating the fast break, you dribble the ball to the middle while your teammates are running on the side(s) of the frontcourt, and then you simply launch an unguarded three-point *UniShot* layup and continue to run toward the basket to rebound.

  When the shot is good, you can get back quickly to defend. When the ball touches the rim or board and bounces out, you and your teammate running toward the basket at side can out-rebound the defender in a two-on-one situation. You and your teammate have the advantage of facing the basket and having speed to jump. The defensive rebounder can only box out one offensive rebounder, and he is actually sandwiched. These are high-percentage offensive rebounding opportunities even when you are shorter than the defender. Remember, both of you are facing the basket and have more momentum than your defender. The greatest advantage is that you know where your missed shot is bouncing to.

  After getting the offensive rebound, either you or your teammate can make a power move to make a second-effort shot or draw a foul for a plus-one play. This long layup fast break is called a three-point fast break.

- **Side shots.** Low-hand *UniShot* makes it easy when you are shooting on the sides and there is no angle to make a bank shot. The *4u1* alignment of *3fz* enables an accurate layup from zero angles on each side. There are high-arc *UniShot* layups good for behind-the-board shots when you have to shoot in the last seconds of the time clock.

- **Dynamic moves.** You can drive past your defender and make a quick step low-hand *UniShot*, or make a slow long step to make more adjustment or decision to pass or fake, then make a *UniShot* layup.

  It is also efficient in catch-and-shoot situations. As soon as you catch a pass in transition, you can launch a low-hand *UniShot* in a quick *RFT*, or one-hand-only process, and you still have the options of dribbling or passing.

  The low-hand *UniShot* is powerful with a sharp turnaround layup. It has a smooth combination of spin moves, either under the basket or away in the peripherals.

- **Reverse layups.** Applying the index finger in low-hand *UniShot* enables you to shoot easily around the basket by rolling the ball to basket-favoring sidespins. A reverse layup can be extended to a straight-arm layup on the other side of the basket, regardless of using the backboard or not.

- **Behind-the-board layups.** For low-hand *UniShot*s, behind-the-board shots are just extra-high-arc layups, and they can be made dynamically in the game situations. They yield amazingly good accuracy since the higher arc produces more accurate shots.

Future Shots

If Universal Shooting Mechanism is the future of basketball shooting, the low-hand *UniShot* will be the future of *UniShot*s for its dynamics, quickness, and variety. The low-hand *UniShot* listed above is a standard zero BBR shot. BBR stands for *ball-body-rim* angle; it is the angle of two lines: one line is from the body center to the shooting ring finger, and the other line is the body center to the basket.

Figure 21. Advanced *UniShot*s

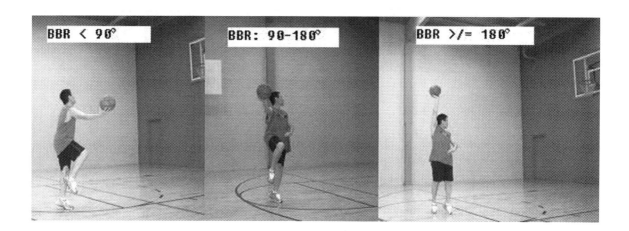

With different arm positions to the body center, the variety of low-hand *UniShot*s could range from 0 degree BBR to >180 degree BBR. A ninety-degree BBR low-hand *UniShot* looks like a half hook or half layup. Shooters must keep their hands' *4u1* alignment to the target in shooting variable BBR shots. With the ambidexterity of *UniShot*s drained *3fz* mechanism, low-hand *UniShot*s are actually covering whole shooting scopes of the body, three-dimensionally.

Mini FSC

Mini *FSC* is the smallest Finger-Spring Cup of a hand. It is applicable to all *UniShot*s, particularly for the underhanded shots. Since the weight of the ball is mainly on *MAP* of the shooting hand, the shooting power and control are more dependent on *MAP*. In mini *FSC* with fully adducted thumb, *MAP* has the longest arm to apply shooting force onto the ball. In this form of *FSC*, *MAP* is more passively abducted, with mainly the fingertips controlling the ball, and the fingertips of the thumb and index finger are also actively holding the ball. Mini *FSC* gives the shooting hand more dynamic power and control in wrist deviations and finger twists.

Low-Hand *UniShots* Advantages

Low-hand *UniShot* is the future of *UniShot*s, also the beginning of *UniShot*. It is convenient for everyone to start to learn *3fz* mechanism by shooting the low-hand *UniShot*. Most children and women have relatively small hands; the best first move for them is the underhanded shot, since it has the exact body posture of a layup. This approach works also for established players; many of them are good shooters with the regular shots, since they do not need to change their shooting right away. In addition, from learning the *3fz* mechanism, they will have much-improved layups with better accuracy and longer ranges. The professional players should go this way too; it adds pure value to their games. After they are confident with *3fz* mechanism and low-hand *UniShot*s, they might start to learn up-handed shots.

Low-hand *UniShot* has technical advantages over other *UniShot*s:

1. Quick and dynamic—you can shoot anytime in any position when you are moving.
2. Protective—your body shields the shots whenever necessary.
3. Accurate and powerful—you have great shooting control and body adjusting mechanism and great shooting power generation from anywhere you are shooting.
4. Excellent for teamwork, especially in transition games for passing, running, and rebounding.

Low-hand *UniShot* will give youths, women, and seniors more opportunities for joining competitive basketball games. Because the requirements of strength, height, and athletic ability of low-hand *UniShot* are very low, the basketball disadvantageous populations can work on their running and *3fz* ball handling to gain more ability for tough competitions. The game of the future will be more mixed, with more coed games and everyone equally participating. More about the future of the game will be discussed in chapter 9.

Chapter 6

Up-Hand *UniShot* Shooting Variety and Combinations

By applying the *3fz* shooting mechanism in different body postures, stances, and biomechanics, the six basic *UniShot* forms provide technical standards for free throwing, field shooting, and shooting training. In real games, besides shooting free throws, these six shooting forms can be flexibly executed in numerous variations, on either one foot or two, with dynamic combinations of drives and moves.

Universal Shooting Mechanism is adaptable to a large shooting variety and dynamics. Just for static *UniShot*s, without jump or move, there are one-handed and two-handed shots on one or both feet. With ambidexterity acquired by *3fz* symmetric training, *UniShot* can spontaneously be launched by either hand according to the plays. Therefore, it is not possible for *UniShot* to be overplayed on just one side. *UniShot*'s ambidextrous nature allows left-side and right-side shootings, which can be set on one foot, two feet, or the "wrong" foot. Real game run, jump, dribble and pass empower *UniShot*s with high scoring potencies of dynamic shots and combinations.

By commanding *3fz* and precise *4u1*, players will be able to freely apply *UniShot*'s varieties, combinations, and dynamics in competitive basketball games. The fundamental basketball drives, footwork, and moves without the ball are all applicable to *UniShot* applications. With teamwork mentality and great *3fz* passing abilities, *UniShot* will bring highly efficient fast-paced and spectacular basketball offenses.

This chapter will give you categorized applications of five **up-hand** *UniShot* forms. Every move and variety of the following sections can be performed with either your dominant (strong or leading) hand (side or axis) as well as your weak (learning) hand. In other words, you can shoot high-percentage *UniShot* with either the left or right hand in each of the following shots or moves.

TWO-FOOT *UniShot*s

Every time you reach out one of your hands to catch a basketball, from either a pass or a dribble, you automatically use that hand as the shooting hand. After catching the ball, you step up with the non-shooting-side foot and follow with the shooting-side foot squared. Keep the body alignment, which is static shooting-side alignment from the outer heel to the knee, shoulder, elbow, and to the shooting hand's *4u1*.

Catch, set, and shoot are the three stages of the shooting process of Universal Shooting Mechanism. Shooting accuracy is dependent on the quality of your ball control with *3fz* and the shooting alignment in the process. Therefore, mastering *3fz* shooting mechanism and Universal Alignment is vital for all *UniShot*s.

Two-foot *UniShot*s are good for the half-court offense, while one-foot *UniShot*s have more dynamics in transition games. Two-footed shots are well paced and possess static triple threat every time you have the ball. The body-shooting alignment is static, and the shooting postures are vertical.

Chest Shot

Chest *UniShot* starts with chest passing by stressing the shooting hand. You catch the ball with a Reverse-Finger Twist (*RFT*) and pass (or shoot) it with two hands. Instead of passing, release the ball in the middle of the chest with two hands symmetrically. Chest *UniShot* shoots (or passes) the ball asymmetrically, with the shooting hand pushing behind the ball and the non-shooting hand holding the front of it. The setting position of the ball is right on the shooting side of the chest.

The catching hand is automatically the shooting hand. The shots can be released with either one hand or two hands. Two-hand chest *UniShot*s are good for quick releases and passes. Setting the two-handed shots, you maintain the triple threat stance until releasing the ball. One-handed chest shots have long shot push and control, and that yields high accuracy.

Shooting Procedure

1) Catch the ball to chest.
2) Hold the ball in triple threat stance.
3) Lift and push the ball with two hands.
4) Release by *MAP*, and finally off the ring finger.
5) Extend legs, back, shoulder, and shooting arm and hand.

Chest *UniShot*s are effective in game situations such as pick-and-roll, catch-and-shoot, pick-and-pop, quick release, and long-range shots like three-pointers. Having the identical stance of the chest pass, the set of chest *UniShot* is a powerful triple threat. Every time you receive the ball in the perimeter, when no defender is closely pressing you, you should start with a chest shot stance.

One-hand chest *UniShot* is technically the most stable and controllable shot among *UniShot*s. Whenever an open shot in the perimeter is permitted, you should use one-hand chest *UniShot* to launch long-range unguarded shots. Its long shooting push and control produce high-percentage shots. You can bend your knee low to the most powerful pushing (squatting) position, and that gives you *the longest pushing distance from knee high to the highest spring point with one hand release*.

In the pick-and-roll situation, the chest *UniShot* is efficient for the guards to shoot quick releases. It is smooth and fast in shooting runners and floaters even you step on the "wrong" foot, the not-used-to jumping foot (e.g. right foot jump in right-handed layup).

Standing *UniShot*

Shooting Procedure

1) Catch the ball to chest.
2) Two hands lift the ball over shoulder.
3) Extend body by raising calves.
4) Shoot the ball on high arc by one hand.

The standing *UniShot* is an extension of the chest shot. You lift the ball high above the shoulder and release it with one hand, pushing the shot by raising the outer calves. The standing shots can be released with either one hand or two hands.

Although the standing *UniShot* is primarily used for free throws, it has practical applications in various game situations. Without jumping, you maintain good balance and can adjust quickly for the next move. The standing shot is a vital part of triple threat, as you have a pivot foot to maneuver fake, pass, or shot without losing your shooting stance. Back-extension standing shots are effective in the game, especially when the ball is coming after you. One-hand back-extension step-back *UniShot* is hard for defense to react after you made a drive-step fake. The standing shot is also a quick shot in catch-and-shoot, pick-and-pop, draw-and-kick, and quick releases.

Jump *UniShot*

Shooting Procedure

1) Jump up on standing shot.
2) Release high on Finger-Spring Cup.
3) Protect the ball with the non-shooting hand.
4) Follow each shot after landing.

Jump *UniShot* is the most effective, powerful shot among *UniShot*s. You jump up and release the ball high on the shooting hand's *FSC* and can protect the shot with the non-shooting hand.

You can also make a two-handed jump *UniShot*, especially under the basket or in congested situations. With two hands on the ball, you can alter the shot to pass before release or make a double clutch and draw fouls. The two-hand jump *UniShot* covers all game functions of the conventional jump shots. However, one-hand jump *UniShot* is far more potent than the two-handed jump shots in competitive games because of its high release, shooting variety, drive combinations, and protection.

Jump *UniShot*s are frequently used in the games. Catch-and-shoot is the most common play of a jump *UniShot*. You can do a back-extension jump shot when the ball is coming from your far side to your moving direction. Scissors or half-scissors jump shots allow you to launch long-range shots with your back toward the basket.

Jump *UniShot*s are powerful in long-range shots. It is practical, fast, and safe to launch three-point jump *UniShot*s when shooters are not double-teamed.

Jump *UniShot* is a quick mechanism for rebounding. Since the body is well balanced on landing, the shooter can cut the open court direct to the basket, *as the shot is challenged on the far shooting side, and the defender automatically loses her box-out position.* With the non-shooting hand free in the air, the shooter can swing the arm, adjust to a quick landing balance, and move directly to the basket. Having good shooting vision allowed by *UniShot*, the shooters are in the most favorable positions to follow up their own shots to catch offensive rebounds. As soon as they release a shot, they know right away if it is a possible miss and the approximate bouncing direction of the ball. Shooters know their own shots best and are the first to verify the misses by their shooting feelings and actually seeing the arc and spin of the ball.

Rear-Catch

Figure 22. Rear-catch shot

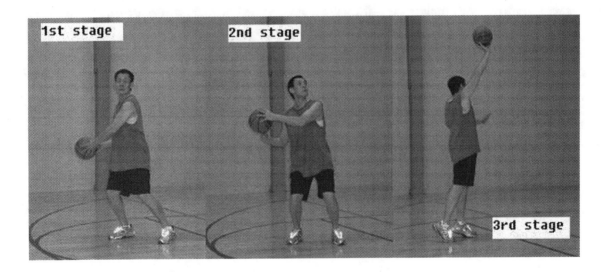

Shooting Procedure

1) Keep body low and shoulder high to the basket.
2) Catch the ball low and far at back.
3) Turn and step in for standing, jump or scissors *UniShot*.
4) Use the other hand for protection.
5) Fake if necessary.

Rear-catch *UniShot* has the best shooting protection, and it is highly effective in combination with other shots and moves. The rear-catch shooting mechanism is deceptive, protective, and three-dimensional.

Shooting protection is not a new concept in basketball, since centers often protect their hook shots with the non-shooting hand near the basket. In *UniShot* processes, just like in regular dribbling, you can always use your non-shooting (non-dribbling) hand to protect the shooting (dribbling). The key feature of rear-catch *UniShot* is the protections of the entire shooting process: catch, set and shoot, which are three main stages of *UniShot*.

The first stage is the low stage of ball catch at the rear, where the upper position of the ball is to your waist.

- Here you can hold the ball temporarily in your catching *FSC*, with your back toward the basket, and try to step further into the defender's lower floor with the non-shooting side foot to feel the defense.
- You can turn your head and shoulder to maintain good vision of the court.
- The non-shooting hand and arm can be used for protection of the ball, ready to clutch the ball, the second stage of shooting.

The second stage is the middle stage—the ball lift and shot set—and it is the static triple threat stage, where the ball moves from the waist to above the shoulder.

- The non-shooting hand clutches the ball on the top and does a Reverse-Finger Twist, with the shooting hand under the ball.
- Make a fake turn in the opposite direction by stepping the shooting side foot while clutching the ball.
- Turn back and lean your opposite shoulder toward the defender by stepping big to the non-shooting side.
- Then two hands set the ball up at the rear for setting the shot in a triple threat stance.
- The non-shooting hand is on the top of the ball, protecting the ball from slapping.

The last stage is the high stage, the shooting and release stage.

- Avoid defensive prediction by not looking at the rim directly, unless you do shot fakes. Use your peripheral vision to target and maintain direct view to the full offensive court.
- Make a quick swing jab step to the shooting side and turn your body, ready for shooting push.
- Lift the ball straight up with the shooting hand at the rear on *FSC*.
- The non-shooting hand leaves the ball and opens up slightly to protect the shot. You can choose to open the non-shooting hand over your head to fend off hand-in-face interference.
- Jump up with both feet and look directly at the basket to shoot. Follow through with the shooting arm.

Rear-catch *UniShot* is deceptive, with different moves and fakes that are hard for defense to detect. With turning, spinning, stepping, jumping, and hopping, you can make rear-catch *UniShot*s very large shooting scopes. It can combine scissors and high shots for high releases and up-handed shots' width and underhanded shots' depth to launch high quality *UniShot*s.

Scissors Shot

Scissors *UniShot* is an innovative application of Universal Shooting Mechanism in dynamic body movements. It takes full advantages of human kinetics and is potent with its shooting variety, dimension, and timing.

Shooting Procedure

1) Back to the basket.
2) Make a fake turn to the other side.
3) Twist-turn and lift the ball at back.
4) Jump up without moving feet.
5) Shoot at far back.

There are three varieties of scissors *UniShot*s: stationary scissors, half scissors, and jump scissors.

Using **stationary scissors**, you can overpower a closely guarding smaller player or a big player staying low.

- By turning back onto the player with a high passing fake without moving any foot, you can then launch a stationary scissors shot directly over the defenders.
- In this shot, first you keep your triple threat stance; if you dribbled, you still have the option to turn or spin for other *UniShot*s.
- It is the fundament shot of the other two scissors shots.

Half scissors are half-step-back scissors shots, good for fadeaway shots.

- They are practical and powerful when combined with other *UniShot*s, especially with one-hand jump shots.
- Half-step-back scissors jump produces a quick jump, more twisting and swinging power, and high, protective shooting positions.
- It is efficient to shoot a half scissors near the baseline when your body is parallel to the backboard and there is no angle for a bank shot.
- Catch-and-shoot situation is great for the application of half scissors. You can use that half step to adjust your body balance and make shots promptly without compromising shooting accuracy.
- With various moves and shots, half scissors shots dictate single defense.

Scissors jump shot is the shot you do in critical moments, such as clock situations or under the basket in congested situations.

When you catch the ball with your back to the basket, and the defense is pressing you with heavy physical contacts:

- You can make a scissors jump, swirl in the air more than 180 degree BBR, and lift the ball with two hands, then shoot the ball with one hand in the rear, away from defense.
- You do not need to see the basket before you jump; you just jump straight up and turn your shoulder to get a peripheral sight of the basket when you hold the ball high with the shooting hand.
- Then you can have a delayed release scissors jump *UniShot*.

High Shot

High *UniShot*s are spring shots at high-spring point, where the body is straight and the joints are relaxed but not flexed. High-spring point is the highest shooting position of spring shots. Spring shots are launched by applying spring power generated by elastic forces of joints and ligaments, without involving major muscles. There are standing high shots, scissors high shots, and one-foot high shots.

Shooting Procedure

1) Catch the ball with two hands from the back.
2) One-hand spring-clutching the ball high on spring point.
3) Block out defense with the non-shooting hand.
4) Use high swing fakes when necessary.
5) Turn body, lift calves, jump, and shoot.

High shots beat sticky defenses such as bear hug or scissors hand. You control the ball with one hand and lift it high against defensive slapping. The non-shooting hand can help support in clutching, holding the ball high, or simply moving around as a shield to aggressive hands of the defense.

High shots are most effective in playing against small, quick defenders. You protect the ball by holding it high to pass or fake. If they jump, you can simply drive pass them. If they stay down low, a high shot can be launched over them.

One-foot high shot is as powerful as a high riding drive and other one-foot *UniShot*s.

Ear/Head Hook

Ear Hook (BBR = 180°) is a variety of one-hand high *UniShot*s, and it can be one-footed or two-footed.

Shooting Procedure

1) Start with half scissors.
2) Pushing shoot aligning elbow-ear-basket.
3) Jump leaning defense of fadeaway.
4) Extend shoulder and elbow.
5) Release the ball on invert finger-spring clutch with head-pointing to the basket.
6) Arm follows the release by touching the ear or the head.

The *3fz* shooting mechanism with Universal Alignment makes it possible to shoot a one-handed shot with head pointing to the basket as a reference of the shooting alignment. Head and neck direct the shots by back viewing with peripheral vision or referring the backboard to the basket. Ear hook creates a variety of head hook shots by flexing wrist, elbow and shoulder joints.

The ear shot is superb in facing bigger and quicker defenders. It usually combines with scissors move. It is accurate in bad shooting environment that defense covers other possibilities of shooting. Ear shot is advantageous over conventional hook shot in shooting variety, range, and accuracy with more shooting controls and options

Quick Releases

*UniShot*s produce a large variety of quick shots. They could be one-handed or two-handed, and one-footed or two-footed. Universal Shooting Mechanism is an ergonomic, fluent and fast shooting mechanism.

Shooting Procedure

1) Catch the ball by *RFT*.
2) Catch, step-in, and shoot in one action.
3) Arm push, finger release while extending the body.
4) Quick shot follow

UniShot is a natural, time-saving mechanism with its

- low and quick *3fz* catch without swinging the ball;
- shooting on catch without lifting the ball;
- pushing and releasing in one single stroke.

Quick-release *UniShot*s are commonly spring shots in different shooting positions. They use elastic power of fingers, hand, wrist, elbow, and shoulder. Spine, legs, and feet are also involved in short pushes. Quick releases are also touch shots of jerking joints and ligament movements. Since the body-shooting alignment and control are executed by the joints and ligaments, spring shots are fast and accurate.

There are also powerful quick releases with muscle involvement. When you are against physical contacts or under the basket, you need to take off strong against defensive pressure.

TWO-FOOTED MOVES

UniShot moves are fundamental basketball moves with the ball, sometimes straight dribbling. Two-foot *UniShot* moves are quite different from the one-foot *UniShot* moves. Two-foot *UniShot*s are usually used in the offensive half court with various team settings, such as pick-and-roll, draw-and-kick, and high-post and low-post. These kinds of moves are powerful but less dynamic. One-foot *UniShot*s are good for transition games, as they have more dynamic moves and shots in fast-paced running games.

Fake and Jump

When you catch the ball facing the basket, you can simply do a shot fake in one direction, then do a spin move or a half spin to launch a two-foot jump *UniShot* or a scissors jump shot. In the situations of leaning the defense with a drive-step of the shooting-side foot, you can make quick drive-fake to the non-shooting side; when the defender reacts with a quick retreat, you simply use the same drive-foot to step back to launch a back-extension jump *UniShot*. Fake and turn *UniShot* is great for must-shoot situations.

For the plays that you drive along the baseline underneath the backboard to the basket, you can make a stop and fake; when the defender moves the arm up, you can simply jump up and use your outer hand to shoot a jump *UniShot* over the defender. Or in the same situation, when you sense the defensive help is coming, you drive and fake aggressively to make the double-teaming defenders leave their heels, then you spin out to jump and shoot a regular or a scissors jump *UniShot*. At that moment, you can also decide whether to shoot or pass.

In common plays of moving to the baseline near the corner, you can do a fake drive or fake shot to the middle court and dribble once, with or without a spin move, to the baseline and make a base two-foot jump *UniShot*. It is a safe shot, since no defensive help comes beyond the baseline. You can also fake with a hesitation dribble and wait for the defender to come on you and draw a foul on shooting for a plus-one play, or you can continue to dribble and drive along the baseline to layup.

When you are corned by the double-team and your teammates are far away, you can make a power fake drive to the defender in the middle court side, then do a quick spin to launch a half scissors jump *UniShot* or simply a full scissors jump without spin. In this situation, when time and space are allowed, you can do the same move as spinning to the corner to shoot a regular jump *UniShot*. In case your shot is altered, it will go out of bonds for your possession, but most likely, you will draw fouls in the situation, since they have to jump up to challenge your shots because your shooting hand is beyond the baseline.

Peripheral Moves

Mixed with one-dribble drive and shot or drive fakes, *UniShot*s can do many damages to the defense and create unchallenged shots for the offense. The potency of *UniShot* moves attracts defensive helps and double-teams. The average offensive players can play draw-and-kick in the perimeter just as big players do in the low-post positions.

UniShot moves in the perimeters are usually fake-and-turn or drive-step moves. Fake-and-turn moves start with your back to the basket against defense. You can do drop step and turn moves to either side for one-hand jump *UniShot*s or scissors shots, fake-and-shoot for back-extension shots, turn-and-twist for scissors shots, or fake-and-spin for jump *UniShot*s. Drive-step moves directly face the defenders and the basket, and they include the drive-step jump shot, drive-step straight drive, drive-step crossover, straight-drive jump shot, crossover jump shot, and step-back jump shot.

Moves beyond the Arc

These are three-pointer fake-and-jump *UniShot*s. It is hard to double-team a shooter beyond the three-point arc. These moves and shots can be used against man defense. When the defenders are less mobile or small, these moves are efficient and yield high-percentage three-point shots. Rarely with big and fast defenders, since the floors are open, is it easy for the offense to maneuver, especially in the crucial times such as clock situations, timely three-pointers, or drawing double-teams or fouls.

Turnout Jump

The existing shooting method requires players to shoot behind the ball, and it allows the defense plenty of time and space to challenge the shots. *UniShot* breaks the norm by allowing players to shoot in front of the ball where it's well protected. When the inside court is congested, you can simply catch the ball outward and make a turning jump and launch one-foot or two-foot turnout jump *UniShot*s. Turnout jump *UniShot* is very potent for three-pointers. When you are inside the three-point arc and have to make a three-pointer for your team, a turnout jump is the most effective way of doing it.

Turnout to the Baseline Corners

It is the safest turnout jump *UniShot*; since defensive help is absent also, the shot cannot be overplayed. Just like a hook shot, high release of *UniShot*s with jump is difficult to challenge. The players can make instant decision easily to shoot a turnout jump to the baseline when the defense is on middle court or a baseline drive. If you make a shot, it is likely you would draw a foul or have a plus-one play, since the shooting hand and the ball are on the far side of your body and opposite the defender.

Turn back to Side

With either a spin move or regular turn, you can easily use open floors; turning or spinning one or a half step away from your defender, you can make a quick-turning jump *UniShot*. The defense has hardly a chance to catch up with you to challenge your shots. If you turn your head and use peripheral vision before the jump, you will know exactly where the defense is and how they react on the move. Then you can decide whether to do a quick jump or to fake and shoot.

Drive and Turn

Combined with one or two dribbles, you can just turn back to the three-point ranges to shoot, usually a jump *UniShot* or scissors jump. The turnout jump is good for back screen and shooting behind a teammate. While your teammate stays behind you high in the perimeters, you can make a drive to the basket, turn your body, and dribble carrying the ball behind your big teammate as a shield or screen. You simply jump to shoot over your teammate whose arms are straight up in a

V shape. You can drive and turn in both directions while you have your peripheral vision to the defensive presence.

Run and Turn

This move is good for *runout and turn* catch-and-shoot. If you defender is chasing you closely, you can make a hesitation fake and turn, and pick a safe side to shoot. If the defender is two steps away, you just turn and jump straight up.

Hop Step

Hop-step application gives *UniShot*s great shooting scopes. Players with great leaping abilities will benefit the most. With a drive step or one dribble, they can jump a *crosscourt hop* to anywhere in the width of the court and launch a two-foot jump *UniShot* from there, mostly in three-point ranges. When you drive or catch a pass along the sideline to the baseline, you can hop to the baseline to launch a safe baseline shot or a corner three-pointer. *Hop and turn* is a powerful move for catch-and-shoot whenever and wherever you are not closely guarded.

Catch-and-Shoot

Catch-and-shoot is a specialty of *UniShot*. Since the ball is caught by *MAP* in *3fz* mechanism, *UniShot* catch-and-shoot is a swift, smooth, and dynamic process that gives the offense dominance in making timely shots. The *3fz* ball-handling mechanism significantly increases players' passing abilities and accuracy, so catch-and-shoot becomes ever more frequently used in team scoring combinations.

Depending on where the passes are caught, shooters can automatically adjust to the most efficient *UniShot* for that catching position. Three-dimensional *UniShot*s can be launched with all ball catching positions, and you still can combine the shots with moves and steps, or even one-footed jump.

Post Up

Post-up *UniShot* is now good for average-sized players to post up in the perimeters just like a seven-footer posting up near the basket. Of course, you still can post up low near the basket, but you will face more defensive challenges. A post up in the perimeters, especially in the three-point range, will give defense tremendous pressure, since they have to double-team you if your defender can't even challenge your *UniShot*s.

Posting up in the perimeters, you should maintain good court vision and be a triple threat all the time, and you can shoot a rear-catch *UniShot* anytime you want it.

ONE-FOOT *UniShot*

One-foot *UniShot* is applying the *3fz* shooting mechanism with one-foot jumping. It emphasizes dynamic balances and coordination of contralateral bodies and muscles; it also enhance mind-body or brain-hand cross connections of both contralateral axes. One-foot *UniShot* is good for running or transition games.

One-Step Shot

One-step *UniShot* starts with a two-hand ball clutch low at the shooting side. Then you step into the defensive zone on the heel of the opposite foot. Lift the ball in protective fashion and jump with stepping foot. Shoot the ball on *FSC* of the shooting hand. The non-shooting hand leaves the ball and moves up to protect the shot or shooting vision.

One-step shot is quick, sudden, and protective. It can be used as a leaning shot, good to draw fouls for plus-one plays. When one-step shot is used in catch-and-shoot situations, it is almost impossible for defense to challenge. One-step one-foot *UniShot*s are good for short ranges in congested environments and for long-range shots such as three-pointers. It could be a step-out three-pointer, which needs good body coordination, or a step-in three-pointer, which is common in catch-and-shoot transitions.

One-Step one-foot *UniShot* is a smooth-moving shot. Its sudden jump usually makes the defense out of sync, and they can hardly react to the shot. The extended contralateral body with jump gives the highest release of *UniShot*s.

Shooting Procedure

1) Two hands clutch the ball on the shooting side.
2) Step up with the opposite foot on the outer heel.
3) Turn, jump, and shoot with one hand.
4) Protect the ball with the non-shooting hand.

Figure 23. One-step shot and floaters

Runner

Running shots are practical and effective in transition games. *UniShot* ambidexterity enables you to shoot dynamic runners anytime with any hand in running-game situations. Runners are usually one-foot, one-handed shots that are fluent and accurate.

Running layup is an up-handed layup running directly to the basket. This shot can be varied to a floater, a quick release, or a delayed shot.

Cutting runner. You can simply drive cut the court to launch a crosscourt running *UniShot*. It is powerful when you cut the court and get a pass for a quick one-step catch-and-shoot, and it leaves the defense no time to react.

Baseline runner. If you drive or receive a pass along the baseline to the basket, you can simply shoot a runner with the hand opposite the baseline. It gives you great shooting space and timing even if there is a zero angle to the backboard.

One-hand catch. In the curve or crosscourt running shots, you can use your non-shooting hand to fend off the defense and protect the whole shooting process while you single-handedly catch a pass and shoot a running shot. When the pass is high enough, the shooter can make a high catch and lift to shoot, and the defense cannot do anything against it.

Three-point runners. A running *UniShot* can be launched from anywhere along the three-point arc. It gives big players and players with great leaping abilities huge advantages by shortening the three-point distance in the air. If a big player jumps up from outside of the arc, he might not be able to dunk the ball but can shoot a running *UniShot* in the air less than three meters away from the rim. That is a quite makeable shot. The other advantage is that after the shot, you are still running toward the basket to rebound a possible miss. It is the best chance for the shooter to catch a rebound after the long shot misses since the ball will bounce on the ring relatively high, and the shooters will have time to adjust their running toward the ball with the greatest momentum to jump.

Run Back and Turn

One-footed runners are so dynamic that you can run to any direction or anywhere on the half court and launch a one-hand *UniShot*. It is effective when a shooter runs from inside the three-point arc to the outside in driving or receiving an outlet a pass; the shooter can simply catch the ball, turn to either side and step outside the arc, make a turning jump, and shoot a *UniShot* in the air. It is not only quick and sudden but also hard for defense to anticipate. With the shooter has side vision on the defense, he can decide where to run and which direction to turn. It is a highly makeable last-second shot.

Faking Layup

Making two long steps, fake with the first step and shoot on the second step. Faking layup is powerful in driving to basket, and good for making passing or shooting decisions. There are many ways of doing fakes to distract the defense.

Shooting Procedure

1) Low drive-catch.
2) Shot fake on big sticky step.
3) Jump on smaller step.
4) Shoot and release.

Floater (figure 23)

3fz mechanism allows *UniShot* to catch the ball quickly, which sets an easy floating shot before the defender can come up to interfere. Since you can shoot with either hand and jump on the opposite foot, it is difficult for the defense even to recognize the shot. When you have good body balance, *UniShot* can float on the "wrong foot," or on any foot. Floaters can be low-hand *UniShot*, depending on the catching and defensive situations.

Shooting Procedure

1) Drive for a layup.
2) Quick catch and do a first-step release.
3) Follow the release to rebound.

Curve Shot

Curve shots are the runners around the court focusing on the basket. When you drive around the paint or three-point arc and the ball is kept outside, it is a good situation to shoot a curved runner. The other hand can open in front of running direction to protect the shot.

Curve-out fadeaway. When you are running a curve with the defender kept inside, it is safe to shoot a one-hand fadeaway *UniShot*.

Run-out three-pointer. You can run a curve and step out of the arc to launch a curve three-pointer.

Reverse curve. If the defense is overplaying on one side, you can simply run a reverse curve and shoot a one-step shot.

Fly-out curve. If the game situation needs you to shoot, you can run a curve out to the sideline or baseline to launch a fly-out *UniShot*.

Curve in. When you drive along the baseline underneath the basket, you can run a curve and make a one-foot turning jump zero-angle *UniShot*.

Curve shots can be mixed with low-hand *UniShot* or half hook. A curve shot is difficult to predict and easy to combine with catch-and-shoot with a pass.

Side Shot

Side shots are drives to the far side of the basket and are usually two-point shots. *UniShot* side shots can be launched using the backboard or direct to the net. Opposite of the curve shots, side shots drive a reverse curve away from the basket. At the end of curve, the side shot is released in the form of a one-footed ear shot. The drive steps of side shots are big, low, and powerful; with two big drive steps, the defense will be left out of sync by jumping up too early.

ONE-FOOTED MOVES

Catch-and-Shoot

One-footed catch-and-shoot is athletic, and it needs good balancing skills. Since a pass can come to you at any angle and height, you need to catch the ball and adjust your body balance to have a one-step or two-step shot. Once you can control your balance and steps, one-footed catch-and-shoot can be launched near the basket, along the baseline, in the perimeters, or even behind the board. No matter where the pass is coming, you should just keep your orientation to the basket, step up, jump, and shoot.

Big Two Steps

One-foot *UniShot*s are powerful in drive. You drive and catch the ball with your shoulder leaning toward the defender, step big, and fend off slapping with two hands holding the ball at the body side; then you make the second big drive step to jump. You can launch a high shot or a side shot.

Rollover

Rollover is a powerful move driving against a smaller defender or through traffic. After you clutch the ball low with two hands, you can lift the ball high to drive with a big drive step through traffic or simply over the top of a smaller defender. In shooting, you jump with a smaller step to launch a one-footed shot.

Post Up

Based on two-footed post-up shots, one-footed shot is launched on quick one-foot jump *UniShot*.

DRIBBLE-AND-DRIVE COMBINATIONS OF ONE-FOOT AND TWO-FOOT *UniShot*s

Crossover

Two-foot crossover *UniShot*s have wider moving scopes, while one-foot *UniShot*s more quickness and dynamics.

Simple cross. Simple cross is the situation where the defender is guarding you with one foot in front. You can drive a simple cross to the defender's front foot side, step your front foot across the defense, and launch a one-step one-hand *UniShot*. It is a misstep for the defender to retreat with both feet, and he is incapable of jumping to block. If you want to draw a foul, you can use a two-footed jump shot with a jerk fake.

Quick cross for three-pointer. A quick cross is launched when you already trick the defender to move the opposite direction, and then you drive a quick crossover to shoot a one-foot or two-foot *UniShot*.

Delayed catch. When you finish a big crossover drive, you can decide to have a quick shot or a delayed catch and make a big hop step and then launch a two-foot *UniShot*. Delayed catch is a triple threat and can also be opted to a one-footed shot.

Reverse turn behind a back screen. Back screen is a screen set by a teammate in the peripherals when you have the ball inside with a defender guarding. You can drive out around the pick set by the teammate and launch a turn around *UniShot*, usually with a one-footed quick shot. When the defender runs around the other side of the screen, you can do a reverse turn to launch a two-foot *UniShot*.

Cross and hop. Crossover with a hop step allows you to shoot wide-range *UniShot*s. The cross and hop *UniShot*s can cover the whole width of the court. Hop steps are for two-footed jump shots only.

Delayed three-point cross. Delayed crossover can be launched outside the three-point arc as needed. The shots can be one-footed or two-footed.

Back Cross

Back cross is the move when your back is toward the basketball against the defender. You can use the back cross with a fake to shoot a one-foot or two-foot *UniShot*. Back cross shots can cover wide scopes of the floor. It is practical when you have the ball at the baseline with your back to the basket; you can make a fake step to the middle of the court, then turn and drive a back cross toward the sideline to launch a one-foot or two-foot *UniShot*. If the defender is closely pushing you, you can sense it with your leg and use a back cross drive to the basket for a layup.

Step Back/Aside

Inside out dribbling is the basic skill of making a step back or aside *UniShot*. When you make a fake drive step the opposite direction and dribble inside out, you can push the opposite fool to step back or aside, then catch the ball to launch a two-step or one-step *UniShot*. You can also initiate the body contact and control your balance to step back or aside and shoot. The step back/aside covers wider open courts in combination with a hop, including the three-point ranges.

Cross Legs

Cross legs is a simple dribble that can help you get rid of a sudden step-in pressing defense. Every time you dribble cross legs to the side of the defender's front foot, you have the option to do a quick one-step shot, a hop-out two-footed jump, or remain a triple threat stance by continuing to dribble.

Leaning shot. Leaning shot is launched when the defender is pressing you. You make a close body cross-legs dribble and then step with the opposite foot close to the defender and jump up, leaning toward the defender for a one-foot *UniShot*. Or you can step in with the shooting-side foot and launch a two-foot leaning *UniShot*.

Hop step. Cross legs with a hop is made by pushing on the shooting-side foot and jumping out to the open floor. You can drive cross legs to observe the defender's posture. When the defender is quick on move to the shooting side, you can then make another cross-legs and hop away to the opposite side. The cross-legs hop step has great rhythm as a tic-tac-toe move of jump, catch, and hop. Of course, you can delay the catch for one-foot or two-foot *UniShot*s.

Quick three-pointer. In the perimeters, you can make a cross-legs dribble and drive or hop to the outside of the three-point arc and then launch a quick three-point *UniShot*. The shot can be launched one-footed or two-footed, according to the defensive presence.

Behind-the-Back

Behind-the-back dribbling by *3fz* mechanism has technical advantages of being quick, hidden, and deceptive. It is uniquely combined with *UniShot*s for quick hidden catches and protective shooting or deceptions, and it produces a variety of power shooting moves with one-foot or two-foot *UniShot*s.

With behind-the-back dribble, you can do one-step quick shot, long hop shots, leaning shots, reverse turns, spin moves, back crossover, three-points, and other moves.

The *3fz* mechanism allows one-handed secure control of the basketball, and *FSC* enables you to do hand deviations and pronation in dribbling. In addition to its protective features, it gives behind-the-back dribble technical edges with greater maneuvering scopes. The *3fz* behind-the-back ball-handling will be the prime technique for *3fz* dribbling skills.

Spin Move

UniShot spin moves look similar to regular spins. Compared to the conventional spin shots, spin *UniShot*s have wider ranges and shooting protection. The ambidextrous *UniShot*s can be launched in the perimeters, one-handed or two-handed, one-footed or two-footed, up-handed or underhanded.

The Spin *UniShot* has excellent dynamics that involve and coordinate all major muscle groups, and it is a great tool of *3fz* symmetric training.

Reverse Turn

Reverse turn is a move in changing turning directions. It involves defense detection, shooting hand switch, and delayed catch in a run-out *UniShot*. If a turning shot to one direction is anticipated and then overplayed on the shooting side by the defense, a reverse turn move is needed. Reverse turn shots can be any kind of *UniShots* in combination with all the dribbling moves. It is powerful in a needed three-pointer and clock situations.

Chapter 7

3fz Conditioning and Symmetric Training

The *3fz* mechanism leads to a simple way to play basketball. Its unique training and conditioning include the physical and intellectual integration of players' athletic talents and academic educations, which benefit youths the most. It explores innate resources that everyone has equal possession of. Learning and practicing *3fz* is a methodology of enhancing physical, mental, and intellectual development in young people and improving physical and mental well-being for adults. It reinvents traditional symmetric training with cross-connect corrective learning (described in the later section of this chapter) that allows players to acquire ambidextrous sports skills and athletic systems in relatively short time.

By learning *3fz*, you will not only master this unique skill for basketball excellence, but you will also learn to understand and command your own body. It will give you lifelong benefit for your physical and mental wellness. The *3fz* methodology of training and conditioning can also help the athletes of other sports improve their skills and athletics. Learning *3fz* is a refined and detailed process, and it is not just physical or skill training; it also entails scientific learning, logical thinking, and mind-body harmonization.

If you want to master *3fz* in a relatively short period, let's realistically say at least two years, the first thing you need to do is get enough knowledge of your physical body, especially your hands. The anatomic and biomechanical understandings of your hand, the second most important resource of your body after your brain, are vitally important in learning *3fz*.

The structures of the hand, bones and joints, ligaments and muscles, and nerves and blood vessels, are the basic knowledge you need to learn. The feelings, functions, movements, and coordination of these components of hand are more complex, which you need to comprehend and experience along with your academic learning. In order to excel in basketball by mastering *3fz*, you must have solid knowledge of physics, mathematics, biology, and physiology to understand biomechanics and kinesiology of your hand and body. Educated training is the key of *3fz* success in accordance with the Individual Revolution Plan included stated at the end of chapter 1.

In the next step, you need to learn how to use your hands smartly, the same approach as playing the piano, but not to abuse them. Your hand consists of small bones and joints and fine muscles, and thus it takes long periods of systematic training to build up their mass, strength, and skills. **Patience**, **Relaxation**, and **Rest** are the three virtues of *3fz* training.

Patience

Learning *3fz* is more of a mental process than a physical one. First, experiment in your own body with scientific knowledge, sensing, recognizing, and understanding the components, movements, and coordination of wrist, hand, and fingers. Second, execute correlative learning methodologies systematically between the leading and learning hands. Symmetrical skill transfer takes time and efforts.

Traditional sport training and physical conditioning principles are essential but not sufficient for *3fz* learning. Hard work is not enough; the process should be focused in educated training.

You might feel anxious or even frustrated for not getting the results you want at the beginning. You should not be concerned, as the initial stage is always slow in *3fz* training. In this stage of learning, relaxation and rest are more important.

Relaxation

The *3fz* finger practice is not pleasant the first day of training. If you have played basketball for a long time, you might feel awkward or difficult using *MAP* as your primary fingers to control the ball. The more years you played conventional basketball, the more uncomfortable you will feel with *MAP*. This kind of difficulty will disappear when you overcome this initial learning obstacle and get ever-stronger ring fingers and little fingers by continuing well-relaxed practices. Anyhow, for all the people who have practiced *3fz* for the first time, this problem is brief, lasting for only a day or two.

Using proper relaxation drills is important during the first week of *3fz* practice. They can help you reduce the initial discomfort, establish quick touching connections among the fingers, strengthen *MAP* more efficiently, and most importantly, avoid injuries since the finger muscles are delicate and sensitive. Relax your hand and fingers frequently, more in the start. There are many relaxation techniques and drills you can do in the intervals of *3fz* drills. Learn to use them to relax you muscles, ligaments, joints, and forearms.

Strict alternation (one by one) of both hands is the law of *3fz* training. Always start a drill with your dominant hand and then change to the weak hand right after one try of the drilling skill. This gives both hands active rest and corrective learning in both strong and weak hands (sides, or axes).

Rest

Whenever you feel any discomfort or abnormity in finger, hand, wrist, or arm, you should stop *3fz* drills and do relaxation exercises. If the pain or discomfort persists in the next drill, you should stop practicing and rest your hand until it recovers 100 percent. You will learn the signals of hand and fingers in *3fz* drills. In the end, you will understand more and more of your body: hands, fingers, muscles, ligaments, and nerves. You can best train yourself if you understand your physical body, because only you have instant feedback from the inside of the body.

LEARNING *3fz*

The principles of *3fz* learning are patience, relaxing, and rest. Take time to simplify and amplify every single action, sense the feelings and touches of the fingertips and skins of your hand, and decode the signals of muscles and nerves, understanding and thinking about their identity, functionality, involvement, and coordination.

Fundamental understanding of the hand's anatomic structures will be a great asset in the *3fz* learning. With ball-handling practices, you should:

- Get to know the components, structure, and systems of the hands
- Understand their functions, movements, and mechanisms
- Establish the feedback or signaling systems between your mind and hands

OK-Sign Dribbling—"A Good Beginning Is Halfway to Success"

This is the very first, fundamental drill for everyone to learn *3fz*. Form an OK sign with thumb firmly touching the tip of the index finger, like a precision grip. Index finger is relatively straight; the space between thumb and index finger takes a form of an "eye" rather than an O. Extend *MAP* with straight MP joints and relaxed full abduction. Keep the wrist relaxed and flexible. Always alternate dribbling hands to refresh muscle memories in each drill.

Touches of Ring Finger

Start to dribble, by OK-formed *MAP*s, a basketball with a soft surface, a leather game ball, or a slightly deflated ball of synthetic materials. At the beginning, just gently dribble and poke the ball with the *MAP* fingertips. This drill will initiate the feelings of touches of *MAP* on ball surface, especially of ring finger and pinky. Try to recognize the vertical forces and angles (inward or outward) of the ball applied to your *MAP*.

The second drill is to softly dribble the ball with the *MAP* fingertips vertically down. Slightly flex the IP joints and extend the MP joints backward when poking the ball; allow more control with the finger pads and make longer ball contact. Take advantage of the round surface of the basketball and roll the ball by the abducted *MAP* with more pressure between the middle finger and ring finger. This way, you develop stronger *MAP*.

The third drill is to use more of the *MAP* finger pads between the MP, distal IP, and proximal IP joints in dribbling. Practice progressively and sense the ball touches clearly; first touch the ball surface with the fingertips, then the distal pads and the proximal pads until the ball reaches the MP joints. Apply more force to simple up-and-down dribbles; lastly, let the ulnar side of the index finger, OK signed with thumb, touch the ball. A good dribble is letting the ball roll from the fingertips to the pads and then to the MP joints, with index finger guiding. This establishes the *MAP* joints coordination and the index finger involvement.

Strengthen MAP

Now dribble the ball by slightly changing direction, using the radial side of the index finger. The wrist is involved in the dribbling actions actively, with constant flexion, extension, and deviations. The DTA is active in pronation and supination, *MAP* abduction and adduction, and associated movements of metacarpals and intrinsic muscles. This drill will strengthen muscles and ligaments of *MAP* and the palm, including lumbricals, interosses, and hypothenar muscles.

Alternate dribbling hands to develop *MAP* strengths and skills symmetrically. Apply more force by flipping wrists for harder dribbles. Try to do the exact same actions with the weak hand right after the strong hand's lead, and to have instant mirror learning of muscle memories and coordination.

Exaggerate body, arm, and hand movements by amplifying the dribbling actions in slower paces and larger scopes. Copy the muscle memories from the strong side to the weak side and try to process them in your brain. Feel the joints, ligaments, and muscles for their involvements in each dribbling action and recognize the signals each part of your body sends to you.

Comprehensive Dribbling

Dribble the ball with OK-formed hands just like regular dribbling with all five fingers. The ulnar side of the index finger might be used to practice. You can do crossover, cross-legs, behind-the-back moves, spin moves, hesitation or dynamic triple threat, step back or aside, or any kind of fancy or non-regulated dribbling. This drill emphasizes *MAP* controlling the ball in hand, arm, and body coordination.

Relaxation

In the beginning stages, you should relax your fingers once during every fifteen minutes of dribbling practice. It prevents any negative impacts to *MAP* in the early training. After three weeks of training, the intervals will be longer, depending on the feelings of each individual. Stop training when you feel any discomfort in *MAP* and then do the relaxation drills.

Figure 24. Relaxation drills

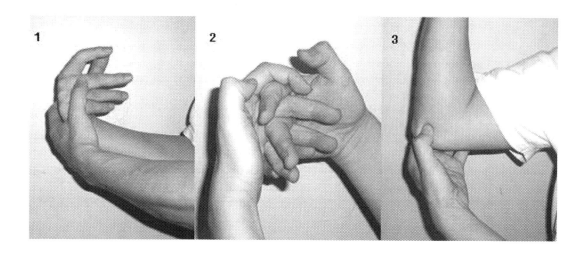

Relaxation Drill 1: *Passive Flexion of the MP Joints*

Phase 1. Using the thumb of the massaging hand and holding the hand being massaged at the back, press the MP joint of the proximal phalange bone of the ring finger and make the fingertip touch the palm three times, counting to three seconds each time, with gentle vibration. Do the same three times on the little finger. Then come back to the ring finger for the same massage, and then to the middle finger and index finger. The final press is to hold and press the four fingers together, make the *MAP* fingertips touch the palm three times.

Phase 2. Do the same sequence in phase 1, with the fingertips touching the carpal crease of the wrist without turning the DTA.

Phase 3. Turn the DTA in supination in the pressing massage process, letting the *MAP* fingertips gradually touch the radial side of the forearm.

Phase 4. This phase is a combined exercise of relaxation and stretching of tendons, muscles, and hand bones and joints. Use the radial side of the whole thumb of the massaging hand to press the whole proximal phalange bone on the proximal IP joints, letting the fingertips gradually touch the middle portion of the forearm.

This drill is effective in relaxing the whole hand, especially *MAP*, in the finger joints, tendons, ligaments, and muscles. Since most *3fz* practice is involved in hand and finger extensions, the relaxation is mostly flexions. It restores energy to the hand with relaxed blood flow.

Relaxation Drill 2: *Reverse Finger-Intercross*

Intercross your fingers of two hands reversely, with palms facing down. Press the MP joints of both hands against each other. First, hold each other fingers loosely and do up-and-down rolling friction movements of MP joints by flexing and extending the wrists and pressing the hands. Second, do radial and ulnar deviations of the wrists ten times and let the MP joints move against each other like two gear wheels. Lastly, repeat the first stage and extend the arms' moving ranges until the elbows touch.

This drill relaxes both extension and bending muscles of the three fingers as well as wrists and forearms. Then change the finger intercross to the other (not habitual) holding cross for more mental and physical relaxation.

Relaxation Drill 3: *Elbow Care*

Massage the blood point (concave skin) between the funny bone and elbow, and press it firmly till feeling sour in the elbow. This drill relaxes the whole forearm and the hand muscles.

FSC Formation

After OK dribbling, conscious and active ball touches, and control of *MAP* are established, you can use all five fingers to dribble, catch, pass, and shoot. Finger-Spring Cup formation allows fluent and safe one-handed ball control.

Thumb Support and Coordination

Thumb passively supports the ball, and index finger helps control and adjust ball in the dribbling, passing, or shooting processes. *MAP* first touches the ball in catching or dribbling. The *MAP* fingertips scoop the ball up to meet the supporting thumb and assisting index finger, forming an *FSC*. This action is the combination of wrist radial deviation, palm pronation, forearm swing, and a twist of the DTA. The primary purpose of the complex yet dynamic combination of hand and arm activities is to establish and calibrate Universal Alignment in hand. A *4u1* aligned *FSC* can suck and hold the ball for momentary triple threat without killing the dribbling.

Index Finger Assistance

The index finger is to passively hold the ball and actively guide the ball in changing direction and twisting and rolling the ball. The index finger could actively control the ball when it is not perfectly aligned with *4u1*, and more importantly, the index finger helps reestablish the hand's *4u1* alignment.

FSC Ball Control

The biomechanical law of *FSC* is *4u1* alignment. *FSC* with *4u1* controls the ball independently in the following situations: dribbling, one-handed pass, and one-handed layup or shot. Practice separately for changing ball-moving directions by flipping the wrist and ulna rolling while releasing. Use *FSC* clutching the ball in *RFT* with the other hand, lifting up for shot set, and shooting one-handed.

Universal Alignment

The thumb-to-ring-finger alignment is the innate neural and biomechanical connection of the human hand. It is not difficult to establish the biomechanical association between the ring finger and thumb in different ball-handling drills. The first drill is to have a strong and active ring finger, and get used to touching the ball first with the ring finger. It is flexible and sensitive with its direct association with ulna mobility and neural connections with other fingers.

Internal Neural Connections of 4u1

In dribbling drills, first use a basketball with a soft surface in order to push harder with *MAP* in dribbling and reducing the impact of passive pressure of the bouncing ball. When the dribbling *MAP* has good control of the ball, it will automatically meet the thumb for *FSC* formation.

The ring finger is the center of all three of the hand nerves. The palmar connection with the median nerve, motor connection with the ulna nerve, and the extension connection with the radian nerve are spontaneously built up during the various dribbling actions. The stronger and more sensitive *MAP* you have, the stronger connection and more active association you will build between the thumb and ringer finger.

Adjustable by the Distal Transverse Arch (DTA)

In *3fz* conditioning practice, the DTA connects all five digital rays and has great flexibility in prehension and power grips, hand pronation and supination, and finger extension and flexions. A strong and flexible DTA will enhance *FSC* stability and *4u1* precision. There are many other methods than ball-handling exercises to obtain strong DTA; they include active abduction hand exercise with resistance, separated finger extension or flexion exercise, and metacarpal stretching.

Universal Alignment has slight variations for different ball-handling releases. On the end of supporting thumb, the ball is rolled along the upper curve (edge) of the thumb tip to form four *4u1* alignments for different ball-handling purposes. The other end of the alignments is the radial ring finger, and it remains unchanged.

1. **Dribbling *4u1*:** thumb's lower radial tip on the skin of the protruded distal IP articulation
2. **Passing *4u1*:** thumb's upper radial tip on the nail corner
3. **Low-hand *UniShot 4u1*:** thumb's middle upper tip
4. **Up-hand *UniShot 4u1*:** thumb's upper ulnar tip on the nail corner

Dribble and Pass 4u1s

The dribbling *4u1* is primarily used in continuous dribbling actions without dynamic triple threat. The passing *4u1* is for more accurate long passes or curvy passes with direction changes.

The *3fz* dribbling and passing have the closest *4u1* alignments in hand, which are more toward the radial distal thumb, since the quickness is more important than accuracy in the dribble and pass. Oftentimes the dribbling and passing *4u1s* are interchangeable. When dribbling with a dynamic triple threat, the passing *4u1* should be applied for the readiness to pass or the transit to the shooting *4u1s*. The same when a quick pass is needed: the dribbling *4u1* is used.

Figure 25. *4u1*s

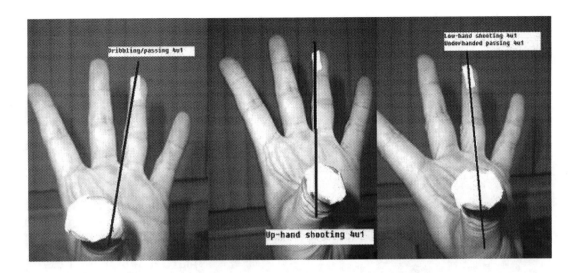

Shooting 4u1s

The shooting *4u1* alignments are more precise than those for dribbling and passing; therefore, they demand more training for its importance in the game. Shooting *4u1*s are obtained by adjusting the DTA in the combination of prehension grip and power grasp.

In the formation of *FSC*, *MAP* rolls the ball up to meet the index finger and then the thumb to form an *FSC*. The thumb first touches the ball on its radial distal tip, where the *4u1*s of dribble and pass locate. In the dribbling and passing *4u1s*, the thumb is slight abducting but not opposing. For the shooting *4u1* alignments, the thumb starts to abduct farther for low-hand *UniShot* and oppose fully for up-hand *UniShot*.

Precise 4u1 Transition to up-hand UniShot

1. In the process, the ball is rolled up on the upper curve of the thumb's tip, ulna-wise by opposing and abducting the thumb and distally to the *MAP* fingertips.
2. In the same process, the DTA turns in the same direction of the rolling ball by hyperextension of *MAP*, where the three fingers have bigger abductions.
3. With full opposition, the ulnar distal thumb tips support the ball on *FSC*, in which the thumb directly aligns with the ring finger and the geometrical center of the ball, establishing the shooting *4u1* alignment.
4. With *RFT* clutch, the non-shooting hand presses the ball on the opposite side to ensure the precise shooting alignment and optimal *FSC* size for the corresponding shot.

Ulna Roll

Figure 26. Ulna rolls

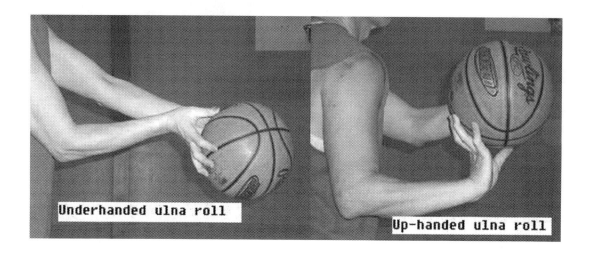

As Universal Alignment is gradually being established, ulna roll is a good drill to condition the hand, especially *MAP*, for strength and skill in calibrating the shooting alignment. The drill is performed with upper arm close to the body for either underhanded or up-handed ulna rolls.

Underhanded ulna roll. Hold the ball in *4u1* of *FSC* in front of your body, with the elbow sticking to the rib. Twist the ball on *FSC* inward by pronating the forearm to the position where you can stably control the ball. Then flip the hand up with a quick supination to toss the ball. Release the ball in *4u1* without generating any sidespin.

Up-handed ulna roll is more difficult and needs the other hand's assistance. Just like a shot set of up-hand *UniShot*. The supporting hand presses the ball on top to set it firmly in the shooting hand's *FSC*. The DTA is twisted outward by a passive hyperpronation of the holding hand. The wrist is now fully hyperextended and the ball pressed down to *MAP*'s MP joints. To shoot the ball, you need to flip up your wrist with a supination, rotate the DTA inward, and release in *4u1*. You should not produce any sidespin of the ball in releasing with ulna roll.

Weight Training

Conventional weight training is applicable in *3fz* training and conditioning. But it should be performed with light weights, 70 percent of maximal strength, and high repetitions, at least sixteen reps each set for two sets. The working muscles should cover the whole body, since *3fz* mechanism will involve them all. Your body fat content should be controlled, in the range of 10 to 15 percent.

Lower body training should be emphasized more over upper body, and it will give you more dynamic power. The most recommended workouts are the squats exercises, regular squats or front squats, possibly with full squats, as they will give you more jumping power and driving dynamics. Regular weight-lifting exercises such as lift, snatch, and jerk are good for overall body conditioning.

Figure 27. Carpal roll and *3fz* front squat

Carpal Roll

Carpal roll is specially designed weight training for *3fz* mechanism to strengthen the wrist. This drill is based on arm-chest press on an inclined bench of about forty-five degrees. You should do it with light weights, starting with an empty bar (forty-five pounds), and do warm-ups with the weight for over sixteen reps of regular inclined arm presses.

After about five minutes of rest and drinking water, sit back and put the bar on your upper chest by pressing with the hands under the bar and locking it there. Then lift it up and hold the bar down to your wrist at the first metacarpal stop by actively bending (flexing) wrist forward. After the full stop at the first metacarpal, extend your wrist by bending backward and let the bar roll to the distal part of the palm to the four fingers' MP joints by sticking out the upper arms and elbow.

Lean the bar close to your chest by rolling it gently past the MP joints to the pads of the fingers against the chest. Keep on rolling the bar to the chest and the proximal IP joints, then pass to the distal IP joints against chest. Now let the bar sink against your chest to hyperextend the carpal joints further, including the carpal bone, muscle and ligament, and proximal transverse arch, distal transverse arch, and longitudinal arch. Stop there for a few second, inhale deeply, and start to push lift with the MP joints of fingers first, then pass the joints to distal palm and lift the bar up and continue to roll it to the proximal palm, to the first metacarpal stop, and then lift it up in both arms and exhale.

3fz Front Squat

The *3fz* front squat is a special exercise for fingers and carpals in coordination with upright body posture in squatting. Starting with an empty bar, it should be performed in the following way.

- Stand with the legs about shoulder-width apart, holding the bar with an overhand grip as it rest on the upper chest.

- Inhale deeply to maintain intrathoracic pressure, which prevents the torso from collapsing forward, slightly arch the low back, contract the abdominal core, and bend the knees to fully lower the thighs to the floor.
- Return to the initial position and breathe out at the end of the movement.
- Stick out the chest and raise the elbows as high as possible to prevent the barbell from sliding forward.
- Roll the bar up against the upper chest by pressing it with the hyperextended MP joints of the four long fingers and thumb tip.
- Do the squats in the same procedure and positions.
- Alternate the holding position to relax the carpal muscles.

The *3fz* front squat is the best weight training for *UniShot* postures and shooting powers. It is a comprehensive exercise for most upper body and lower body muscles.

Stretching

Stretching should be performed before training as warm-up and during the training as relaxation. Before the training, stretching should be gentle and light in combination with aerobic exercises such as running and dribbling. A good way to do it is to use an elastic rubber band to stretch out arms and wrists, or you could use a long wooden stick to stretch shoulders, back, and thighs. Stretching before training is mostly for the upper body. For the lower body, a fifteen-minute warm-up with running dribble is good enough.

Mid-training stretching should be performed for every hour of training. A good way is using a Swiss ball to do hyperextension of the back, to relax the upper body as well as the lower body. Stretch your entire body lightly for the first five minutes and then do a full stretch out on the floor or a mat for another ten minutes. Drink plenty of water before and after stretching.

SYMMETRIC TRAINING

The *3fz* specialized symmetric training is a teach-and-learn correlative method (described in the next sections) to achieve ambidexterity, which gives players the dominant edge in playing basketball, especially in shooting *UniShot*s. For other sports, it is also applicable as an innovative approach in training balanced skills and athletics. Symmetric training has been traditionally used for such activities as military training, agriculture works, and martial arts.

In early physical and mental development, symmetrical training helps youths explore their innate resources, have balanced athletic abilities, and enhance mental acuities of recognition, reflection, and logic and intuitive imagination.

In sport competitions, symmetric training is an excellent tool for achieving an extra edge in skills and athletics. The athletes not only get balanced sport-specific skills, but they also obtain well-balanced body dynamics and coordination, with great endurance and explosive power.

For the general public, symmetric training can well be applied to recreational sports or daily activities for active, healthy living. It benefits us in multiple facets of life: injury prevention, physical and mental wellness, and anti-aging benefits.

3fz Cross-Connect Symmetric Training

Basketball employs players' upper and lower bodies symmetrically. Compared to other free-hand sports, soccer players' hands are not actively involved in the matches, and volleyball or handball players are merely using their dominant hands for spiking or shooting. Basketball is the sport that gives its participants the most balanced overall body workout.

Basketball players, different from the players of other sports, have balanced ball-handling skills in both hands. When point guards dribble the basketball, they almost have identical moves and equal ability to drive to the left and to the right. Good centers and power forwards can hook ambidextrously, with either hand by jumping with the opposite foot. Most players can do layups on their strong sides as proficiently as on their weak sides.

They acquired the balanced skills and power by experiential symmetric training. Players spent substantial amounts of time in the practices of dribbling with both hands alternately and shooting hook shots and layups on both sides of the basket with either hand. The traditional symmetric training is about action simulation, and it works for proximate, not precise, skill transfer. It is effective only in short ranges of free ball movements such as dribbling, layups, or hooks near the basket.

However, *3fz* symmetric training distinguishes itself from the traditional symmetric training in the following aspects.

First, the *3fz* symmetric training is *precision training*, while the traditional is the proximity approach. The free-flying distances of the ball in dribbles, hook shots, and layups are quite short, usually less than three feet (one meter) of dribbles, six feet (two meters) for layups, and ten feet (three meters) for hooks. If you control the ball in proximate directions with less power, you can keep dribbling possessions or make layups and hooks within the distances. On the other hand, the basketball rim is so big in size that it can encompass three and a half basketballs. Even if your shot hits the rim, the ball has a good chance of rolling in or bouncing in such a big basket.

The *3fz* symmetric training is about precision and internal transference of the ball-handling mechanism. Universal Alignment, a precise ball control mechanism, ensures fine skills and power transfer between the teaching and learning hands (sides, or axes). It empowers both hands/sides with balanced power, sharpness, and dominance in dribbling, passing, and shooting. The *3fz* symmetric training is the foundation of *UniShot* training; it facilitates achieving ambidextrous, accurate *UniShot*s.

Second, conventional symmetric training is completely experiential. Players are training their weak hands or sides in simple simulations of the actions of their strong hands. There is no training system or principle to follow. This kind of free approach lacks coherence with nerve systems, muscle memories, and brain connections of leading and learning axes. It produces only proximate power and control; therefore, the ball's free-flying distances are very limited. On the other hand, players must train their skills separately for dribbling, layups, or hooks. If their strong hands do not possess good skills in one category, their weak hands can't learn either. That is the reason many big players cannot dribble the ball and many small players cannot hook.

The *3fz* cross-connect symmetric training is a systematic approach based on precise *4u1* alignment and the **teach-and-learn coherence principle**. It unifies symmetric training for dribbling, passing, and shooting; players do not need to learn them separately. In *4u1* alignment, the learning axis can acquire the fine skills systematically through multiple connections of nerve systems, muscle memories, and brain interactions from the leading axis in accordance with the teach-and-learn coherence principle. It generates improved power and control for both leading and learning axes.

In *3fz* and *UniShot* systems, our body and mind interact in complex **cross-connected** systems or axes. We have two hand-brain connections:

1. Left hand to right brain—relates to intuitive thinking
2. Right hand to left brain—relates to logical thinking

For upper-lower limb connections:

1. Left hand to right foot—relates to running and one-foot *UniShot*
2. Right hand to left foot—relates to running and opposite one-foot *UniShot*
3. Left hand to left foot—relates to the left shooting-side alignment for two-foot *UniShot*
4. Right hand to right foot—relates the right shooting-side alignment for two-foot *UniShot*

Cross connection is a *3fz* term. It refers to the integration of left and right hand-brain-limb connections in symmetric training by strict left-right alternation. In *3fz* cross-connect training, the **two contralateral hand-brain axes**, the teaching and learning axes, are cross connected, and the **four limb connections** are cross connected. The hand-brain cross connection will trigger intensive intellectual activities, while limb cross connections will enhance balanced athletic systems and brain activities.

In *3fz* symmetric training, the interactivities among the systems include dynamic body movements, active brain instructions, automatic muscle memories and skills transfer, active simulation and passive copying, and correlative correction and improvements among the axes and sides.

Third, in *3fz* driven *UniShot* symmetric training, it is the **power transfer**. You can stably and solidly involve your body and apply forces of all major muscles freely since you have the ball precisely aligned in *4u1* and firmed held by *FSC*. You will be able to use both your hands to dribble the ball with more control and variety, throw accurate long passes, and shoot accurate *UniShot*s that can be excellent substitutes for all existing shots.

Teach-and-Learn Co-Improvement Philosophy

It is also called teach-and-learn cohesive principle or teach-and-learn correlative method.

This is an ancient Confucius philosophy. If you teach a good student a subject, you have to be prepared by studying the subject. If one day the student becomes an excellent scholar in the subject because of your teaching, you might have improved yourself to the level of a professor of excellent scholars.

Teach-and-learn philosophy is applicable in *3fz* symmetric training. The philosophy deduces a teach-and-learn coherence principle in learning systems between the dominant and weak axes of the human body. The teach-and-learn coherence principle refers to internal knowledge and skill transfer of human bodies and brains.

For example, you can throw a javelin with your strong arm ninety meters direct on the target. In the teach-and-learn coherence principle, you should be able to train your weak arm by mirror learning from the strong arm and throwing the javelin about the same distance on target, since they are trained symmetrically in the same way. And during the process, your strong arm is also practicing for the perfect throwing form, since it needs to correct itself in teaching the weak arm. The result will be that you can throw even farther with your strong arm, let's say one hundred meters, right on target.

Ambidexterity Training

Mirror Learning

Mirror learning is the simplest way of acquiring ambidexterity. When you finish one drill action with the dominant hand, you do exactly the same action with the weak hand to mirror the leading hand. In the process, your teaching (leading, dominant, or strong) hand is doing your best performance, with clear and significant muscle memories and brain connections for any particular basketball drill, and then it is followed by your learning hand trying with the best effort to mirror the images and actions done by the leading hand.

This is more of a mental process than a physical drill. You should concentrate the muscle memories and brain connections of each drill by transferring the mechanisms from teaching axis (hand to foot biomechanical connection) to the learning axis. The procedure, body and muscle involvement and memories, the pace, the feelings and touches, the thinking with educated knowledge, and environmental feedback, are all actively involved in the mirror learning process.

Amplified Actions

Action amplification is a fundamental concept in mirror learning. It is the same methodology of learning to play piano, though it is asymmetric practice. At the beginning, you play a simple melody with much slowed-down paces and light keystrokes on the piano. First you want to establish hand-eye coordination of simple music notes to piano keys. Then you will try to hit the right key with the right finger in the right sequence and pace. Your mind is thinking of this melody that you've heard many times and trying to incorporate your eyes and hands for playing it like music, not a physical exercise.

In *3fz* symmetric training, handling the basketball is a creative process. The advantages of *3fz* mirror learning over piano playing is that we already have a leading hand with good skill, muscle memories, and mind connection. We need only to amplify the action we drill with the leading hand and transfer the skill, the muscle memories, and the mind connection slowly to the learning hand.

The amplification of a skill can be conducted in three ways: **time amplification, space amplification, and action exaggeration.** Let us take an example of *3fz* crossover dribbling.

- **Time amplification.** First you dribble the ball at a slow pace to allow more time for muscle memory and brain reflection. Don't worry that you might carry or hold the ball for a longer time between dribbles as the *3fz* technique permits this.

- **Space amplification.** You increase the moving ranges of the dribbling action starting with an up-and-down dribble of the dominant hand from the far back side of the body. Catch the dribble slowly with *MAP* of the dominant hand and roll it up to the MP joints, then add index finger to help *MAP* form a four-finger cup to scoop up the ball in a forward movement. Open your thumb with extended elbow to meet the ball to form an *FSC*.

  Step forward with your foot of the dominant-hand side to fake a straight drive, with a radial deviation of *FSC* and a shoulder shake to stress the fake action. On stepping on the floor with the faking foot, imagine that the defender is moving to the direction of your fake drive and then do an *FSC* pronation and a wrist flexion to redirect the ball to the opposite direction. Your stepping foot makes an ankle drop turn and pushes with the outer calf to move your body to the opposite direction, and your *FSC* sweeps the ball in *4u1* alignment to the opposite hand. In the middle of the body, your dominant hand shoots the ball out to the receiving hand with *MAP* to intended safe spots on the floor. The ball is released off the ring finger with the extended arm and wrist. Your learning hand is ready to catch the ball using the same process of the leading one.

- **Action exaggeration.** If you have problems in *FSC* formation and *FSC* pronation, exaggerate the dominant hand action by stressing the difficulties in static drills, such as practicing with the ball against a wall or your own body, or with a smaller ball. Do not worry whether it is a realistic dribbling action; the sole purpose of ***action exaggeration*** is to assist the learning hand in commanding each fine step of the skill from the dominant hand.

Internal Transfer of Muscle Memory

Try to establish muscle memories with your dominant hand with significant consciousness of each action and exaggerate the action with stressed forces for stronger feelings. These kinds of memories are recorded by your muscles and are simultaneously impressed into the frontal lobe of your brain. Action amplification builds body coordination and move scopes; you can use them to concentrate on the detailed actions, especially the ones you have difficulties with. The learning axis follows the exemplar action of the dominant axis by copying the muscle memories to itself and simultaneously to the contralateral frontal lobe of the brain.

This cross connection of the alternated teach-and-learn activities will bring automatic learning correction and teaching perfection. Along with this praxis, not only does your weak axis enjoy fast learning paces, but your dominant axis will improve itself to a new high level of perfection. In this internal transfer of muscle memory with cross connection, both sides of your body will gain greater power and balanced skills of higher levels.

External Success Check

You might feel confident in cross-connected mirror learning with power and skills transfer, but you still need to check your practical performances externally. Ball throwing distance and accuracy, extreme moves and fast actions, and game situation testing are all criteria of learning success. Demonstration to experienced training partners and video recording with computerized analyses are all good checking methods.

Increased Complexity

After successful mirror learning with simple skills, you can increase the complexity of the drills. The fundamental skills and body conditioning are vital for more complex skills learning. In every training session, you should start with the simple drills first and gradually raise complexity when you have total confidence with the fundamental ones.

Competitiveness and Sharpness: Power and Control

Power and control are balanced in the mirror learning objectives. With fundamental muscle memory transfer, you should master the basic drills to develop the subconsciousness of using the learning axis in the game. When the habits are built up to a certain level, you should be able to automatically alternate both of your hand when the situation requires. This is the prerequisite of developing competitive sharpness, as you are mentally and skill-wise prepared.

Self-Consciousness of Physical and Mental Involvement

Movements and Functions of Bones, Ligaments, and Muscles

First you need to understand your hand anatomically, because you need built muscle memories among them with active, conscious brain assistance. You should be able to tell the hand components, systems, and functionalities by just moving your own hands; then handle a ball to get feedback of drilling actions. It builds up a static self-consciousness of your own hand.

Internal Dynamics of Major Hand Nerves, Ligaments, and Muscles

You should practice your hand and fingers' functionalities with all the anatomic movements: flexion and extension, abduction and adduction, supination and pronation, and deviations. Identify the hand mechanisms and coordination of nerves, muscles, and ligaments. This is a good way to train hand muscle and ligaments with useful skills while you get to know hand dynamics.

The 3fz Conditioning and UniShot Training Principles

1. Always switch shooting hands
2. Dominant hand first and mirror with the other hand
3. Use only spring powers and keep body balanced
4. Amplify each drill in staged actions
5. Use active reflexes for each action
6. Alternate one foot or two foot, long or short ranges, and static or dynamic shootings
7. Follow every shot to rebound

Facilitated Training

Two-basketball dribbling is the most efficient way of symmetric training by instant mirror learning. Juggling practice is an excellent way to develop agility, hand-eye coordination, and sharpness of both hands.

Two-hand racket sports training produces exceptional effects in acquiring ambidexterity. You may use two tennis rackets, one hand each, to hit a tennis ball against a wall. It gives you instant, dynamic, and subconscious learning from strong hand to weak hand. As you persist in the practice for an extended period, with half an hour drill each day, you will develop balanced skills and strength in both hands.

Symmetric Therapy

Symmetric therapy refers to cross-connect symmetric exercises in our daily lives. It will bring tremendous benefits to the physical and mental wellness of the general public, just as it already works for me. The objectives of symmetric therapy are

1. to transfer internally the skills from dominant hand to leaning hand;
2. to improve dominant hand's skills with more power and control;
3. to promote general health with active living.

The therapy can be conducted in daily life activities such as dining, writing, or any hand-involving activities. They should follow the same principles:

- Instant mirror learning from dexterous hand to awkward hand. Always use the skilled or dominant hand first and then switch to the weak or learning hand in doing the same action. Transfer fresh muscle memories directly to the learning hand. Get into the habit of doing everything with strict alternation of both hands.
- Learn a skill to change to the new habit. The process includes the muscle coordination, fluency, quickness, sharpness, and thinking process of the action's physical and mental engagements.
- As is human nature, learning is always from slow to fast, soft to hard, simple to complex. A solid start is most important in new learning. So take your time, allow your space, and be patient with the learning pace.

- Amplify the actions in terms of time, space, intensity, and thinking processes. Exaggerate the moves and actions so that you can stimulate your brain cells for more vivid, specific memories.
- Have a real mirror, do testing, or have an observer for external corrections.
- The standard of ambidexterity is the ability to perform a task spontaneously with the weak hand.

The cross-connect symmetric therapy can promote public health tremendously. You will prove it by doing it yourself. You will not only find yourself much quicker in thoughts and actions than before, but you will be in better physical condition as well.

Everyone can perform *3fz* symmetric therapy in creative ways. Switching the knife and fork while dining should be good a start. Recreational activities are best for doing symmetric training or therapy.

Chapter 8

3fz Advantages and Benefits

The *3fz* one-hand ball-handling mechanism is a paradigm shift in basketball offense. For a new game, *3fz*-driven *UniShot* substitutes the conventional, static two-handed squared-feet over-the-head shooting with its one-handed dynamic shootings. With its core component of *3fz*, *4u1* unifies basketball offensive skills of passing, dribbling, shooting, and catching. Therefore, players do not need to train each skill separately anymore as far as the conventional offensive skills. *UniShot* is a natural yet robust basketball shooting mechanism that outperforms, with its exceptional shooting accuracy and range, any of the existing scoring methods: jump shots, layups, hooks, and any other shooting throws.

The *3fz* mechanism reinvented symmetric training for ambidexterity. With its cross-connect symmetric training, in a relatively short period, a basketball player will be able to, with either of her hands, shoot accurate *UniShot*s in professional three-point ranges. Combined with drives and moves, ambidextrous *UniShot* makes it technically impossible for single defensive coverage to challenge, or even to interfere with the shots. The defense team has to double-team a *UniShooter* in the perimeters, especially in three-point ranges, each time she catches the ball. That will bring never-faced challenges, thus system changes, to basketball defense.

With *3fz* conditioning and training, especially cross-connect symmetric training, occurs enhanced physical and mental development as well as learning abilities in children. It will empower basketball players with dominant, ambidextrous basketball skills and excellent athletic systems, and lead to longevity of sports life. It will also bring tremendous health benefits to the public and help prevent numerous health problems among middle-aged and elderly adults.

HIGHLY EFFICIENT BASKETBALL OFFENSE

In *3fz* revolution, basketball offense will change entirely. The shooting, ball handling, and team settings will be played with new techniques and concepts. The existing offensive basketball skills will be obsolete. Players won't be active in the games without mastering *3fz* and *UniShot*. It is a gospel to the basketball world since everyone will have opportunities to compete in high-level games, as long as they can run, jump, and master the *3fz* mechanism.

All-Around Ball-Handling Skill

Three conventional basketball skills—dribbling, passing, and shooting—are technically independent and need to be trained separately. Players may have talents in one or two of the skills. It is rare that an individual possesses all three of these talents. Great players work on their weaknesses, and they put extraordinary effort and training time into mastering needed skills.

The *3fz* mechanism brings **standard, unified techniques** for all basketball-handling skills of dribbling, passing, shooting, catching, and any kind of ball touches. In *3fz* training or conditioning, when you train for one skill, such as dribbling, the other skills, like passing and shooting, will improve simultaneously because all ball-handling skills are integrated in the *3fz* mechanism and its components: *MAP, 4u1, FSC,* and ring finger control.

The *3fz* is an innovative tool to explore uncultivated resources residing in our hands, bodies, and brains. Universal Alignment is a unique ball control mechanism of one's hand, the most sensitive liaison of the median and motor ulna nerves and biomechanical unity of thumb and ring finger. This alignment coordinates all five fingers, palm, and wrist, and directs joint and muscle movements. With this innate aligning ability, *3fz* handles the basketball in a simple, unified way, by using one hand for all ball skills. Whether you dribble, pass, or shoot the ball, you always maintain ball control in *4u1* alignment. The *3fz* with its *4u1* is the standard mechanism that manipulates the ball in exactly the same process: *MAP catch/release* and *4u1 control,* for executing any skills.

The *3fz* mechanism helps basketball players explore and develop their natural talents and abilities in training and competition. With *3fz* cross-connect symmetric training, they can obtain ambidextrous basketball skills and well-balanced athletic systems that can't be achieved by regular training. With its unique concepts and mechanisms, *3fz* conditioning can be extended to other ball-handling sports and the cross-connect training to our daily fitness workouts.

Fast and Secure Ball Catch

Basketball offense always starts with ball catch to get ball possession. No matter what game situation or body stance you have, you always try to catch the ball with your *MAP* touching the ball first, because they are *more flexible and extensible* than thumb and index finger.

The *3fz* catches the ball by first touching with *MAP*. The three fingertips form a flexible curve for soft and safe ball touches. Mechanically, the ball is unlikely to slip away from the dynamic, sensitive fingertips of *MAP*. Considering the elbows are usually slightly flexed, *MAP* reaches the highest, farthest, and lowest points with extended arms. Therefore, *MAP* has *the largest reaching scopes* to catch a round basketball.

MAP is the most dynamic, powerful combination of radian stability and ulna mobility. In a good first serve in tennis, the ball is flying at a speed of 130 miles per hour (about 200 kilometers per hour) and lands accurately in a small serving area. The main power and control generated by the entire body are transferred through *MAP* to the racquet and onto the tennis ball by the facilitation of radian stability and ulna mobility of hand.

The *3fz* ball catch is *the securest way* of catching the basketball. With *MAP* and its dynamic ulna association, an offensive player can catch the ball low and far away from the defense. The addition of the index finger assists the catch and *FSC* formation, increasing security and dynamics of the ball catch.

UniShot Ball Catch

- *UniShot* **ball catch is secured by** *3fz* from the low, far, and back sides of the body. In the same stance, the body sets as a shield between the defense and the ball. *FSC* formation allows one hand to hold the ball momentarily without killing continuous dribbles for a dynamic triple threat. In *3fz* dribbling, *FSC* sucks the ball with the index finger and thumb on the top, thus it is not likely to be called palming.

- *UniShot* **catch is deceptive.** As you catch the ball behind your body, it is difficult for defense to notice. By maintaining good body postures of triple threat, you can use head and shoulder to fake, and flex wrist and elbow for any possible ball direction changes.

- *UniShot* **catches are hidden and protective**. Your body in the middle blocks the defense's view of the ball. Your free hand and arm set a cushion to keep a defender at a distance, and you can use your free hand to clear the path of ball movement or protect the ball while catching.

- **It is a fast and smooth process.** *UniShot* catch has excellent combinations with dribbles and passes because of its uniformed body posture and *FSC* ball control. It is a quick catch since *MAP* controls the ball at the lowest bounce height for the earliest possible touch. Ulna mobility allows the ring and little fingers to react and move with great dynamics. It is difficult to detect swift, hidden, and dynamic *UniShot* catches.

UniShot Clutch

UniShot clutch is the start of the shooting process or the static triple threat, and the end of the dynamic triple threat.

After the ball catch, the non-shooting hand actively meets the ball on *FSC* of the shooting hand at the back or the side of body. Two hands clutch the ball with a Reverse-Finger Twist and set it firmly in the shooting *FSC*. *RFT* clutch is a powerful shot set that ensures *4u1* alignment and adjusts to optimal *FSC* size.

While two hands are clutching the ball, your shoulder and arm turn to the basket, your shooting-side foot steps in, and you set the shot right after the catch. *UniShot* ball catch and clutch are actually one single quick combination for setting a shot. You are ready to shoot, and the defense essentially has little time to react or move toward the set shot at this moment.

For low-hand *UniShot*s, ball catch and clutch is just one quick bang. That makes the underhanded shooting a nonstop process with fluent rhythm. The whole shot is just one stroke action for ball swing, catch, clutch, and pushing release.

All-Finger Ball Control

The *3fz*-formed *FSC* actively involves all five fingers in handling the basketball. It incorporates flexible *MAP* and stable thumb and index finger into precise *4u1* alignment and accurate shooting and release controls. The hand's joints, bones, and ligaments coordinately generate pure elastic forces onto the five fingertips, where the ball is manipulated with great sensitivity, precision, and dynamics.

MAP Roll Dribbling

With *3fz*, the ball is dribbled mostly with the fingertips. The *MAP* fingertips, pads, and MP joints flexibly touch the ball for changing directions or triple threat hesitations; dribbling is actually a constant finger-rolling process. As a standard process, the *3fz* dribbling consists of *MAP* roll catch, *FSC* control, and *MAP* roll sweeping release of the basketball.

Quick 4-Finger Ball Catch

The *3fz* ball catch is a hesitation dribble of dynamic triple threat. It is a momentary action in a split second of *FSC* ball holding. When *MAP* rolls the ball up with the index finger in a quick radial deviation of the wrist, you can make a shot fake by a jerk lift of the body and a short look at the rim. At this moment, you may decide whether to clutch it with the non-shooting hand or to continue dribbling. This is a four-finger ball catch without forming an *FSC*.

This four-finger ball catch allows your hand a fast transition between dribbling actions. When you continue to dribble in the same side, for instance, inside-out to inside-out or behind-the-back to behind-the-back, you can just do four-finger dribbling without *FSC* formation. If you need to change dribbling actions, e.g., from inside-out to behind-the-back, or alter the dribble to a pass or a shot set, you just do a quick radial deviation and add the thumb onto the ball to form an *FSC*.

FSC Variations

The hand sizes of players are different, not necessarily correlated to their heights. Children grow bigger hands within certain ages during their physical development, and an adult can have wider hands with proper training. To different hand sizes, *FSC* is adjustable; the formation and adjustment is the same technical process for any hand.

FSC has great *flexibility* as well as *stability*, since *3fz* integrates basic functionalities of the five fingers and their associations with radian stability and ulna mobility into a one-hand ball-handling mechanism.

Although the length of the human hand remains unchanged after full physical development, it can be trained to grow more muscles and longer ligaments for **a wider and fatter hand**. The growing areas include DIs and PIs, thenar and hypothenar, flexor retinaculum and palmar aponeurosis, and the DTA. Wider and stronger hands will enhance the *FSC* variations with flexible adjustments for specific ball-control purposes.

The largest *FSC* of a hand is formed by pressing the ball down to the MP joints of *MAP* and the thumb's tip. In this position, the ball has the biggest contact area with the hand—and the strongest power and control in changing directions or twisting actions. This cup is excellent for low-hand *UniShot*s and passes, when the ball is relatively mobile.

The smallest *FSC* is formed on the adducted thumb tip near the top ulnar fingernail corner, the tips of *MAP* and the ulnar tip of the index finger. In this position, *FSC* has the longest lever from the wrist to the ends of the fingertips, for the highest shot set and the most dynamic spring powers. This cup is great for high shots or passes.

FSC sizes in between are flexibly formed by adjusting the thumb. They are universally used in shooting, passing, or dribbling.

Shooting and Releasing

FSC secures one-handed ball control, while the *4u1* finger alignment ensures the accuracy of ball releases. *FSC* is formed strictly with five fingertips, where *MAP* controls *4u1* precision and dynamic ball positions in the shooting process.

Ulna roll shooting. In the shooting stage, the ball is set on *FSC* with *MAP* in back extended wrist positions. On mobile ulna, ring and little fingers turn the DTA outward so that the *MAP* fingertips form a slightly outward curve holding the ball. When you start to shoot the ball, wrist and forearm generate more swing and spring powers to *MAP*.

In releasing the ball on the thumb support, the shooting wrist generates flipping power and applies to the arm of force between thumb and *MAP* (the height of the isosceles triangle) to dump the ball forward. On the thumb and the index finger leaving the ball, *MAP* pushes farther with the powers of the up-dumping wrist, the inward-turning DTA, the lift-pushing arm and back and leg, and swinging back, shoulder and forearm. At the end, the ball is released between the tips of the middle and ring fingers and finally leaves the ring finger.

Maximum Shooting Power and Control

UniShot driven by *3fz* brings significant improvements in shooting accuracy and range. It is the mover and shaker of the revolution in basketball-shooting techniques. The new techniques include *FSC* control, *RFT* clutch setting, *4u1* release, and dynamic body alignments.

In this shooting mechanism, we can coordinate our bodies to work together for exceptional shooting power and control. *UniShot* with *3fz* enables us to generate maximum shooting power and full shooting control for excellent accuracy and precision.

Long Shooting Push: Push Low, Release High

UniShot sets shots in *low body stances*. As soon as the shooting hand catches the ball, the non-shooting hand clutches it and sets the shot low to the knee. In this stance, the shooting push starts from above the knee level, and the release is at high-spring point.

The shooting push is usually along a straight line; however, it can also be a curve according to *UniShot* variety. It is like swimming strokes, where the hand underwater is moving in a curve but pushing water in the same backward direction. Scissors *UniShot*s are perfect examples of curved shooting pushes; great momentum can be added to the shooting power in the process.

Shooting push lasts to high-spring point, the highest shooting position with a fully extended body, where only elastic forces of joints and ligaments are available. The shooting release of *UniShot* is powerful, with *spring power* generated by dynamically coordinating fingers, wrist, elbow, shoulder, knee, and ankle.

The shooting power is controlled by the *3fz* mechanism in the whole pushing distance from above the knee to the toe-tipped straight-body high-spring point. You can add more shooting push by jumping; then the pushing distance will exceed the height of your body.

Full Shooting Control

Five fingers are actively involved in controlling the ball during the whole shooting process. Structured by *FSC* and *4u1*, the five fingertips form a large control area on the ball surface, with a long lever of force between *MAP* and thumb. This arrangement empowers the fingers of excellent sensibility, flexibility, and dynamics to control the ball movements in the shooting process. They can change ball-moving directions, manipulate its gravity centers on hand by wrist deviations, correct the courses of the shooting push, and adjust the shooting power generated by the whole body.

The wrist produces three major controls in the shooting push:

1) The passively extended wrist transfers power to hand and fingers, and adjusts the finger positions for precise *4u1* alignment.
2) It dictates pronation and supination of the shooting hand and ensures smooth and stable ball control of *FSC*.
3) The active wrist shaking with spring power flips the ball at the lever of thumb-*MAP* with optimal speed and power to ensure the ball is released in the right direction, with optimal weight, good arc and spin, and the correct finger order.

The upper arm keeps the elbow close to the body, but not to force it like the conventional shootings. The forearm is flexed before release for optimal ball holding and shot set. When the ball is lifted up, the forearm is vertically straight to keep stable ball control on *FSC*. The shoulder turns to control swinging the arm to shooting direction. The process of arm extension and swing also controls the ball's throwing power and flying curve.

Foot and ankle adjust body-shooting alignments. In one-foot or scissors *UniShot*s, feet and ankles control the timing, pushing, and releasing of the shots. The calves control body balance and ball release. In two-foot *UniShot*s, outer calves generate most control power in the shooting process.

Maximal Shooting Power

The *UniShot* process of shooting power generation is athletic and dynamic. The shooting is a combined power move of the shot put and javelin of track and field events. The ball is shot with vertical pushing of shot put and the horizontal throwing of the javelin. This combined shooting power pushes the ball flying with great speed on high arc. The results of this combined power are long shooting distance and high accuracy. It is a strong contrast to the conventional shooting, which involves only limited pushing of the arm.

Universal Shooting Mechanism involves and coordinates all major muscle groups of the body, including the muscles of the legs, hips, abdomen, back, chests, shoulders, and arms.

- In the **catch-and-set stage**, upper legs, hips, and back are more involved by staying low in triple threat stances.
- In the **lifting stage**, shoulders, back, abdomen, and legs are more active by keeping good shooting postures.
- In the **final shooting stage**, chest, lower legs, shoulders, and the shooting arm have the upmost power generation, especially in shooting long shots.

With its excellent power and control, *UniShot* produces long-range and accurate shootings. The improvements are significant but differ from person to person. It depends on how well players master the *3fz* mechanism with conditioning in *3fz* training.

Full Shooting Protection

The first time in basketball, the whole shooting process can be protected. Since *3fz* enables one-handed shooting, the non-shooting hand is free and can be employed to protect ball catch, shot set, and shooting release. Besides hand and arm protection, *UniShot* sets the body as a shield, fencing up the shooting process. It gives single coverage defense no chance to steal, slap, or block the ball, or even to interfere with the shooting.

Far and Rear Side Catch

UniShot ball catch can be performed in any angle to the body as far as the hand can reach. It is practical and safe to catch the ball behind the body, far away from defense. This way, a defender in front cannot reach to slap the ball, or possibly even see the catch—because your body might block the defender's vision.

Arm, Shoulder and Leg Shield

Figure 28. Protective stance and shooting protection

When a defender is closely guarding you with body contact, it is advantageous to you since you can launch safe scissors or high-spring *UniShot*s.

- By simply staying low and pressing your opposite shoulder on the defender's body, you can shield the shooting-side ball from being slapped.
- You can use the contra pressure of the defender to step out with a dribble and then catch and shoot the ball in one quick action.
- Or you can use a dribble-and-drive combination, such as inside-out dribble and step away, to launch a shot on the far side.
- If the defender's body is pressing on your back, you can have a drop step to fake and jump with the opposite foot to launch a one-foot *UniShot*.

The ball's shooting process is well protected by free shoulder and arm. *UniShot* integrates offense and defense in the shooting process, just as if you had a spear in one hand and a shield in the other hand. With this unique feature, *UniShot* can't be defended without double teaming.

Non-Shooting Hand and Arm Protection

The non-shooting hand can help set the shot with *RFT* clutch or hold the ball in triple threat stance. But the most important role of the non-shooting hand in *UniShot* is to protect the shooting process from catch to final release.

In a one-hand-only *UniShot*, especially in underhanded shots, the non-shooting hand can be used for

1) shielding the defender's hand from coming too close in ball catch (figure 28-A);
2) clearing the path of uplifting the ball for shot; and
3) straightening up to protect the shooting release.

In the regular one-hand *UniShot*, the non-shooting hand can protect the low and high stages of the shooting process just like in points 1) and 3). **In the middle lifting stage** (figure 28-B), the non-shooting hand clutches the ball in the front to secure it from being slapped.

In the releasing stage (figure 28-C), the non-shooting hand can also be used to clear the shooting vision when the defender tries to do hand-in-face interference. The hand should open straight up for shooting or vision protection without committing offensive fouls.

The non-shooting hand protection is also good for drawing fouls. If there is defensive contact to the hand, it should be called as a slapping foul accordingly.

Factors of High Shooting Accuracy and Precision

All-finger control and long shooting push are two major factors of *UniShots'* high shooting accuracy. The *3fz* mechanism involves and coordinates maximal bodies and their movements, and generates the forces and momentum for shooting controls. All these integrate to compose the natural, smooth, and accurate shooting mechanism—Universal Shooting Mechanism. The following are the factors contributing to the high shooting accuracies of *UniShots*.

- *Clean look to the basket.* *UniShot's* shooting stance and posture allow you to maintain good vision to the court and basket. The unique shoulder-side shooting position of *UniShot* diminishes the defense's chances of reaching the ball. If the defender's hand is trying to challenge the shot on the far side, you will have a clean look to the basket.

  It is not practical or logical for the defender to block your shooting vision and leave the shot open. When she tries to do hand-in-face, you can simply use the non-shooting hand to fend it off and clear your view to the basket. Because you have a clean look at the basket and your shot is not challenged, you will be much more confident in making shots.

- *Balanced shooting posture.* In conventional shooting, keeping straight-up body balance is a must. When the balance is not upright, the shooting accuracy is greatly compromised. *UniShot* allows flexible and dynamic body balances. Players have options for dynamic shooting alignment and can easily obtain shooting balance to launch well-coordinated shots.

- *Adjustable shooting mechanism.* *UniShot* driven by *3fz* is flexible, with a large shooting variety. It makes shooting processes adjustable and controllable. The only requirement of all *UniShots* is to maintain Universal Alignment of the hand when releasing the ball. With *4u1* alignment, you can adjust your shootings instantly from up-handed shot to underhanded shot, or from low release to high-spring shot.

- ***Fully controlled shooting process.*** As stated above, *UniShot* is a fully controlled shooting process due to all-finger controls, *FSC* holdings, and *4u1* alignment. *RFT* and ulna roll increase the controls in the shooting release. All these contribute to higher shooting accuracies.

- ***Maximal shooting power and control.*** The shooting power and control generated by the whole body, with maximum muscle involvement and body dynamics, contribute a good portion of shooting accuracy, especially for three-point *UniShots*.

- ***Full shooting protection.*** As the opposite hand, arm, and shoulder help fence off defense, shooters will have more confidence in making shots.

- ***Smooth shooting flow and rhythm.*** *UniShots* have natural, smooth shooting flows in *3fz* mechanism. They are fluent, fast, and powerful, and paced well with dynamic footwork. One-foot *UniShot* is so prompt that it is almost impossible for defense to follow its rhythm. Low-hand *UniShot* is quick and smooth, leaving no time for defense to react.

Team Offense Improvements

The *3fz* and *UniShot* not only give the average individual player dominance over any single defender in three-point ranges, but they also bring more offensive opportunities to the whole team. The team offense will be tremendously elevated in shooting percentage, offensive rebound, assists, and offense efficiencies.

- Since *UniShot* can be launched ambidextrously in wide ranges of the perimeters, it pulls out the defensive to outside the three-point ranges and opens more spaces for offensive team plays such as cut, screen, pass, or any transition play.
- To defend a great *UniShooter* effectively, the defense team has to double-team every time she gets the ball in the perimeters, in order to avoid easy three-pointers. That will leave the offensive team one player open near the basket, and the shooter can make the easy decision to pass the ball to open teammates to score. It will elevate the team shooting percentage and assisting averages.
- A *UniShooter* will open more floors inside the three-point arc. Even when a shot is challenged and missed, the shooter has good position and posture to follow the shot for rebound. As she is not boxed out, offensive rebounders will outnumber the defensive rebounders in any rebounding position near the basket, and there are significantly greater chances to grab offensive rebounds.
- All the conventional offensive strategies, such as low post ups or any power moves, will work more effectively since there is more floor and open space for offensive maneuvers when a *UniShooter* is present in the perimeters.

There are still a lot of other ways to improve the team offense with creative teamwork. The *3fz* and *UniShot* will give the overall dominance to offense over defense; consequently, five players on a team are not enough for defense to constantly double-team a *UniShooter*.

ATHLETIC BENEFITS

The *3fz* mechanism brings significant improvement to players' athletic abilities. For youths, it is overall enhancement in their physical and mental developments. The *3fz* conditioning gives established basketball players improved flexibility, agility, and ambidexterity. In learning *3fz* by playing basketball, senior players can condition themselves for prolonged sports life and active living.

Ambidexterity

Driven by the *3fz* mechanism, cross-connect training reinvented traditional symmetric training. Mirror learning of the weak hand (side or axis) from the strong hand is no more a proximity simulation but a detailed physical and mental learning methodology. It includes muscle memory transfer, fine skills learning, and acquisition of power, sharpness, and dominance.

The *3fz* training stimulates brain-hand connecting and associating activities. The integration of the contralateral associations of mind and body is empowered by cross-connect symmetric training, which is a new methodology of sports training. For overall athletic abilities and skills improvement, this approach can be introduced to track and field, soccer, swimming, or other sports, wherever ambidexterity is useful.

In this book, we deal primarily with basketball training. The *3fz* cross-connect symmetric training is composed of lateral and contralateral system trainings. They integrate biomechanical functionality and physiodynamic coordination of our physical bodies in handling the basketball. The systems to be studied and trained are as follows:

- Ball controlling system—from fingertips to hand and forearm components, structure, movements, and coordinated skills
- Lateral systems—same side: from hands and fingers to upper and lower bodies
- Contralateral systems—opposite sides: left hand, arm, and shoulder to the back, waist, and hip, and to right leg and foot, and vice versa

In *3fz* symmetric training, ambidexterity acquisition is a smooth, spontaneous, and intellectual process. It is a systematic yet creative approach. It sparks your brain activities exponentially with contralateral stimulations of the tactile and motor cortex in your hands' ball-handling activities. You are not only learning in the weak side from the strong side but also improving and correcting the strong side by learning from improper teaching or imperfect skills.

The *3fz* symmetric training is more of a process of sharpness, dominance, and fine skill transfer and collateral or cross-connected improvements than just mirror learning. The expertise and experience acquired during *3fz* symmetric training can be applied to other sports.

Balance and Agility

The *3fz* mechanism involves all major muscle groups and coordinates the body in the dynamic movements of running, jumping, and throwing, as well as turning, spinning, twisting, and pushing.

*UniShot*s driven by *3fz* requires players to have great agility and balancing ability. The *3fz* conditioning can effectively train players with these athletic abilities, which is transferable to other sports.

Prolonged Active Sport Life

The *3fz* conditioning and *UniShot* training are physically demanding but energizing at the same time. The *3fz* symmetric training gives worked muscles active rest and instant recovery. It is all low-stress and low-impact training; one is not likely to overwork any muscle for an extended period of training time. It will significantly reduce wear and tear or overuse in muscles and ligaments; the "No pain, no gain" stubbornness has no place here. Innovatively, *3fz* training cross connects lateral and contralateral systems of the body, which enhances physical wellness and significantly improves mental acuity of players.

The *3fz* conditioning increases bone density and smart muscles (with memories) among youths and adults, as overall dynamic involvements of muscles and bones allows omni-stimulated energy and nutrient transportation to organs and cells.

The *3fz* obeys human ergonomics and is also injury preventive. All these contribute to prolonged sports lives of professional athletes and amateurs.

Enhanced Explosive Power and Endurance

The *3fz* and *UniShot* conditioning and training consist of a series of aerobic and anaerobic physical processes. In the end, you will not only develop balanced skills with great athletics but also grow strong bones and smart muscles. They will give you great explosive power in jumping and shooting, enhancing your cardio functions of lungs and hearts for more stamina. Cross-connect symmetric training also brings athletes the extra benefits of improved endurance of their explosive powers; with a well-balanced and coordinated body, your explosive moves will be more dynamic and fluent, and require less effort.

INJURY PREVENTION

The *3fz* and *UniShot* are unique mechanisms with self-protection and injury prevention. The *3fz* mechanism enables secure one-hand ball handling and saves an extra free hand for self-protection. Self-protection refers to an offensive player's self-defensive postures, along with ball-protection, to protect body from being injured in physical contact. Basketball is an injury-prone sport because conventional basketball offense has no protecting mechanism for its players.

The *3fz* one-hand ball-handling capability allows a player to have a free hand (non-shooting or non-dribbling hand) to help balance the body, set a cushion between her and her defender, and protect the ball and shot or shooting vision. With 3fz, injury prevention is not just for offensive players but also for defensive players, by not taking charges or having unnecessary moves into congested areas.

The *3fz* and *UniShot* are training players for their best athletic abilities for all-around basketball skills. The players can dynamically combine their run, turn, and jump abilities with *3fz* and *UniShot* to launch clean, uncontested, and accurate shots *in open spaces*, where it is less congested, with minimal injury occurrence. *UniShot* gives players excellent shooting abilities in the perimeters and three-point ranges, where the space, vision, and timing are manageable to avoid collisions.

Free Leg, Shoulder, and Arm as Shield

The non-shooting side hand, arm, shoulder, and leg act as shields against defense, and they can structure absorption to possible physical charges or rough contacts. Having one-handed *3fz* ball control on the shooting side, players maintain clear vision to the whole court, and it is easy to detect any defensive help or possible collisions. The shooting sides are changeable to either sides of your body since you acquired ambidexterity in the symmetric training. Therefore, you won't be overplayed on any side; in the same process, you can actively avoid any unnecessary physical contact.

Weight on the Rear Foot When Moving

While in a dynamic triple threat stance with a dribble, you should always set your weight on the rear foot, the shooting-side foot. This way, you can simply push with the foot to drive, or you can step up with the opposite foot to launch a quick one-foot *UniShot*. Your non-dribbling hand opens slightly in front of your body and sets a cushion against defense's pressing body and slapping hands. When you are not facing defense, you can use your non-shooting-side shoulder and leg to detect the defense and block pressing body of the defender. This is the robust *3fz* specialty of *one side as offense* and *the other side as defensive protection*. It is particularly powerful against pressing defense and prevents injuries from hard collisions.

When you are a static triple threat stance, where both of your feet are on the floor, you should set your weight on the front foot, which is the non-shooting-side foot. This allows you to take a quick drive step or simply step in and launch a two-foot *UniShot*. Your non-shooting side hand, leg, and shoulder should be against the defender and fending off the defense's attempting to slap the ball.

Free Hand, Arm, Shoulder, and Leg Protection

In *3fz* and *UniShot*, you have free non-shooting-side lateral body: hand, arm, shoulder, leg, and foot. Besides shooting protection, they also can detect defensive actions, set cushion of physical contacts, absorb the shocks of possible collisions, and avoid charging the defender.

With the free lateral body, you can initialize light contacts to defense to clear the path of dribbling or to open more space for your *UniShot* maneuvers; you can also do a fake catch or switch dribbling hands to become a shooting side.

Free non-shooting-side limbs help keep good balance, move or jump to open floor, and land safely after jumps of dynamic *UniShot*s. All these body involvements will reduce the chance of collisions and falls.

Safe Dynamics of *UniShot*

UniShot and its dribble-and-drive combinations are protective for shooters themselves. The main objective of *UniShot* is to get open for unchallenged shots in the perimeters. It maximizes the use of open floors, where fewer collisions occur. The *3fz*-driven *UniShot*s have technical edges in launching one-handed long-range, protected, dynamic, and accurate shots. The following sections are detailed analyses of the safe characteristics of *UniShot* dynamics.

- ***Step back or aside.*** Step back/aside is a prime move of ambidextrous *UniShot*s, because it shifts the shots far away from defense. The shot is also farther away from the basket, where it is less congested. There are open floors in the perimeters and absence of defensive help. There you can launch your best *UniShot*s with powerful jumps and shots, without considering any physical interference of the court.

  The step back/aside *UniShot*s include up-handed and underhanded shots on one-footed or two-footed jump. All dribble-and-drive combinations facilitate the step back/aside *UniShot*s.

- ***Turn or jump out.*** Faking, turning, spinning, and jumping are basic *UniShot* moves. Final moving directions of *UniShot*s are mostly toward outside floors, away from the basket, where less defensive pressure presents. Ambidextrous hop *UniShot*s with dribble combination would cover the whole width of the basketball court. That means a shooter with good leaping abilities can shoot anywhere in the offensive half court. It significantly reduces the necessity of power moves around the basket, where rough physical contact, hard charges and fouls, and most injuries occur.

- ***Run or drive curves.*** With one-foot *UniShot*s, either up-handed or underhanded, players are running and driving in outside curves from the basket. Off physical contacts or collisions, the centrifugal forces will drag them out, or even fall to the outside open floors. There is no harm for players with these kinds of stumbles or falls.

- ***Run-out or jump-back to open court.*** Run-out and jump-back are other significant advantages of *UniShot*. First, you can make a three-point *UniShot* when the team needs it. Second, the open courts are safe from injury. Third, it is difficult for the defense to catch you and easy to draw a pushing foul after the shot is launched, because it is hard to stop a chase to a *UniShooter*.

Balanced Body

A balanced body is vital for preventing injuries in every sport as well as in our daily lives. It is the only way that we can avoid falling to the ground. A balanced body is also the key in making explosive moves such as shooting a basketball or even making a layup. Unlike conventional shooting, in which a shooter must have straight static balance with two feet squared to launch makeable shots, *UniShot*s allows shooters to have dynamic body balances without squaring their feet.

- ***Dynamically aligned body postures.*** *UniShot*s with *3fz* requires that players move their bodies accordingly to keep the balances to incorporate the dynamic or static shooting alignments for their shots. The *3fz* symmetric training can increase players' balance abilities in all directions. You will have balanced body postures in both clockwise (right) and anticlockwise (left) turns with equal power and skill. Whenever you are running or jumping and trying to launch a shot, you need to keep your dynamic balances; you can naturally launch a right *UniShot* without risking losing balance or falling.

- ***Outward or backward balance control mechanism.*** *UniShot*s have great balance control mechanisms by stepping and jumping dynamically on the open floors. In two-footed jumps, you can turn your body and step in or step out, or step back and jump, or you can twist your body and do scissors or half-scissors jumps. With one-footed jumps, you can jump forward for low-hand *UniShot*s, or you can jump outward and backward for up-hand *UniShot*s. Your legs, back, shoulders, and arms are moving freely and are well coordinated to control your body's balance.

- ***Maximal muscle involvement and coordination.*** As we already discussed above, *UniShot* involves and coordinates maximum body and muscle groups. Their dynamic skills (muscle memories) and involvements produce excellent power and control for balancing the body.

Risks Prevented

*UniShot*s, with dynamic combinations of dribbles and drives, prevent most injuries from happening in competitive basketball games. Not only will your well-balanced athletic body obtained from *3fz* conditioning allow you to cope with risky situations and plays, but *3fz* and *UniShot* mechanisms will also actively avoid possible risks in the game. The following traumatic injuries can be prevented or significantly reduced with *UniShot*.

- ***Step on foot.*** Since you can launch long and accurate *UniShot*s in the perimeters, it is not necessary to try to power into congested areas. You are unlikely to step on defenders' feet, and it will reduce sprained ankles significantly.

- ***Poke in the eye.*** Since the hand-in-face has no effect against *UniShot*s, this weird conduct should be permanently eliminated from basketball games. The hands moving close to face will be deemed purely malicious.

- ***Banging in the knees.*** No need to square feet to launch *UniShot*; you do not need to bend your knees forward against the defensive knees that occur so often in games. If you drive by not facing the defender directly, your non-shooting-side arm and shoulder will provide enough cushioning to avoid direct hard body contact, especially banging the knees.

- ***Wrist and hand injuries.*** The *3fz* training will significantly strengthen your wrist, hand, and fingers. In the new game with *3fz* and *UniShot*, your hand with the ball is always in protected positions away from defense or congestion, and your free hand is moving with flexed wrist and fingers. You usually receive passes to your shooting side on the open floor even when you cut to the middle, since that is a better position to catch the ball for *UniShot*s.

Therefore, there are significantly fewer chances that you would jam, sprain, and dislocate your hand, wrist, or fingers.

- *Other traumatic injuries.* Acute injuries to the shoulder, spine, sacral region, leg and thigh, and eye usually occur because of a fall or contact with another player. The *3fz* and *UniShot* mechanisms reduce the chances of passive body contact with protective moves and shots, and also actively protect offensive players with their own free hands and arms. All these injuries can be well prevented through *3fz* training and conditioning.

- *Malicious off-balance pushes or fouls.* The game with *UniShot* will never be the same as the existing shooting games. The malicious defensive plays will have no place in such a wonderful game. *UniShot*s will fend them off with protective non-shooting side arms and shoulders and make plus-one plays when a foul is committed. Accurate low-hand *UniShot* enables offensive players to layup from a distance to the basket, and it avoids any hard fouls near the basket. The games will not be degraded by hard, dangerous fouls.

- *Harmful plays: scratching, elbowing, knee-kicking, head-butting, and tripping, etc.* *UniShot*s will keep the ball far away from the defense by putting the non-shooting side of the body against the defender, and that will open more space between offensive and defensive players. These are the most common *UniShot* stances, and they will make the dirty defensive tricks obvious—easy for referees to call. Scratching, elbowing, knee kicking, head-butting, and leg tripping are all dirty tricks when the bodies of players are close to each other and in frequent contacts, especially in congested situations.

HEALTH BENEFITS

The *3fz* mechanism and *UniShot* bring tremendous health benefits to basketball players. By emphasizing athletic abilities of agility, balancing skill, and endurance, *3fz* integrates skill training and physical conditioning. It will improve players' performance in basketball games as well as the quality of their daily lives. The *3fz* integrated conditioning and training are suitable for younger players and senior participants, because they are low-impact workouts and improve endurance and agility in people of all ages.

Active Rest and Recovery

Strict one-by-one alternation of *3fz* training gives players' active rests between the dominant axis and learning axis. *UniShot* training shifts muscle-working processes schematically among upper body and lower body, between aerobic and anaerobic processes in static and dynamic movements of lateral and contralateral body axes. These scientifically designed training processes will allow time for active recovery to the body parts and muscle groups. With sufficient hydration and nutrient supply, players will have instant and dynamic recoveries, which will minimize overworked muscles and ligaments, leading to overuse injures.

- *Relaxation interval.* The *3fz* conditioning and *UniShot* training strictly alternate the drills one by one between teaching and learning hands or axes. This training schema gives working muscles constant relaxation. The lengths of relaxation intervals vary from drill to drill. The shortest interval is a cross-body dribble, and the longest is an underhanded shooting move.

- *Aerobic and anaerobic processes.* The *3fz* conditioning is usually aerobic, with low impact to working body. *UniShot* skill training can be aerobic and sometimes anaerobic when jumps, turns, or drives are involved. With well-designed schemes, players can arrange their training in alternation of aerobic and anaerobic processes.

- *Increased muscle, nerve, and brain (left/right) stimulation.* Since our hand movements are directly associated with brain activities in contralateral patterns, *3fz* conditioning with substantial finger involvement will stimulate neural connections between hand muscles and the brain's frontal lobes in the same contralateral axis through the body, such as right hand to left brain. Because *3fz* cross-connect symmetric training is a teach-and-learn system between two contralateral axis and two shooting sides, the training processes will increase hand-brain connecting activities exponentially. In the end, the training will improve brain health in terms of memory improvement, mental health for fast reactions and acuity, and overall physical health for dynamic body and muscles in the sport participants of the general public.

- *Improved muscle memory and coordination.* In *3fz* symmetric training, you have to activate teaching and learning axes alternatively so your muscles will be trained with more intelligence in coordination with other body parts or muscle groups. In mirror learning, you need to transfer your muscle memories from your dominant hand to the weak hand. In the same process, your dominant hand will correct or perfect itself to have a better teaching and greater dominating power and skill.

- *Body-mind harmony.* Your basketball skills are no more just subconscious moves of muscle memories. In *3fz* cross-connect training, your mind consciously directs your teach-and-learn process and has active involvement in the acquisition of new skills of the learning axis and perfection of the teaching axis. It is a new high and harmonized level of coordinating, thinking, learning, and reprocessing processes.

- *Improved power and endurance.* Most players train themselves in the gym for pure muscle growth since it is the quickest and easiest way of self-conditioning to gain physical strength. The flip side of these quick and big muscles is that they don't have any intelligence within, just more mass. There is some usefulness in the conventional games, but not in the *UniShot* and *3fz* reformed games.

With *3fz* and *UniShot* physical conditioning and skill training, players gain intelligent muscle power and skill without gaining weight, which won't compromise athletic abilities such as agility and balancing skills. On the other hand, the intelligent muscles will have more endurance and stamina because they are not structured by simple cell division but by healthy and well-functioning cells. In return, the body with well-functioning cellular organs will give you longevity in sports and life.

- *Symmetric muscle and strength growth.* The *3fz* conditioning, especially symmetric training, facilitates the growth of smart muscles of the learning axis; they are functioning with all the skills and memories transferred from the teaching axis. The teaching side muscles are also well maintained in perfecting their skills. The teaching-hand muscles can gain more power and control by correcting their own defects of a particular skill in teaching the learning hand. In turn, their experiences are then transferred to the learning-hand muscles by symmetric training. Both teaching and learning axes grow well-balanced, intelligent muscles, and they all produce positive biomechanical effects to the body without compromising athletic systems.

Prevent Overuse Injuries

Overuse injuries are mostly caused by biomechanical deformity. Players have a tendency to primarily use their dominant hands or the power moves they have the greatest strength and skill combination to beat opponents. The more they use their strong sides, the more likely they can get overuse injuries.

In chapter 7, we discussed how overuse injuries could be reduced or prevented. The followings are *3fz* benefits in the overuse injury prevention.

- *Balanced body.* In *3fz* conditioning and *UniShot* skill training, players are required to maintain good body balance all the time, either static or dynamic balance. *UniShot* body alignments are multidirectional, with no stress on specific body part, for the knees are the most stressed in squared feet of the conventional shooting mechanics. In *3fz* conditioning and *UniShot* training, players are equipped with great balancing abilities in different body postures and shooting stances.

- *No overload or boredom.* *UniShot* allows players to shoot in a variety of body postures, one-footed or two-footed, running or jumping, and up-handed or underhanded. In training, *3fz* and *UniShot* help build most muscle groups of all body parts by coordinating them in various shooting skills. No particular muscle group is overstressed or overloaded in low-impact and well-distributed *3fz* conditioning. With *3fz* and *UniShot*, training and conditioning are fun, creative, and energizing; your body and mind are in active states throughout the training. You are highly interested and concentrated on training and will not get bored. In these high energy states, you are less likely to have cold injuries due to frequent breaks in hard, boring regular trainings.

- *Stimulated active recovery.* With *3fz* and *UniShot* conditioning and training, you will work your overall body and muscles. The drills are low impact and there is no overload to particular muscle groups. Players might feel tired after a long training, but there is less wear and tear or overuse since *3fz* symmetric training gives the worked muscles instant rest and active recovery. In this situation of tiredness, your body will naturally produce more growth hormones to help recovery while you are sleeping.

- *Overuse injures prevented*

- **Jumper's knee** is due to improper training or conditioning and excessive stress and fatigue. This kind of injury can be totally eliminated by *3fz* and *UniShot* training since you don't need to square your feet for shooting every time.

- **Achilles tendonitis** is the injury caused by repetitive eccentric loading of the Achilles tendon. The injury occurrences can be significantly reduced by *3fz* conditioning, with more balanced body and force distribution in run and jump and *UniShot's* heel-stepping jump mechanism. Ambidextrous shooting alternation in training and games is also a solution to reduce the risks of Achilles tendonitis.

- **Shoulder problems** include impingement syndromes and rotator cuff or bicep tendon strains. Repetitive conventional shooting and rebounding drills can lead to the injury. *UniShot* shooting and offensive rebounding are usually one-handed and ambidextrous, and conditioning with *3fz* symmetric training can also prevent shoulder injury.

- **Shin splints** are caused by impact forces of running and jumping occurring from excessive pronation of the foot. The *3fz* heel land-and-push conditioning can correct the bad habits causing the injury.

- **Hamstring strains** are due to excessive quadriceps training to increase vertical jump height and running speed contributing to a quadriceps-hamstring strength imbalance. *UniShot*s require overall balancing abilities and *3fz* conditioning will train for balanced strength in the lower body; there are significantly more turn and run in a *UniShot* and *3fz* reformed game than vertical jump and hard drives.

Personal Athletic Benefits

The *3fz* conditioning and *UniShot* training will benefit athletes tremendously. The overall workout of the major muscle groups is conducted in an innovative natural mechanism and training methodology. After a period of systematic *3fz* symmetric training, players will acquire not only excellent ball-handling skills but elevate athletic systems.

They will have a quicker first step for driving or moving around the defense, jump higher and longer, turn and spin faster, possess greater stamina and explosive power, and have sharper hand-eye-foot reflection and coordination.

Here is my own athletic experience. In 2009, at the age of fifty-three, after about four years of three hours per day of *3fz* training, I broke all my personal track and field records made when I was a twenty-five-year-old college athlete. The record-breaking events included the hundred-meter dash, four-hundred-and ten-thousand-meter runs, the long jump, and the shot put. My body weight increased by about five pounds, but I now feel more athletic, with improved explosive power and endurance, through these years of *3fz* and *UniShot* training and conditioning.

Chapter 9

Youth Development and Future Games

YOUTH DEVELOPMENT

The *3fz* mechanism will improve the physical and mental developments of youths. It will also enhance their physical and intellectual educations, in and out of school. The *3fz* conditioning and training provide intensive physical activity and learning methodology—exploring the resources of the human brain and body, and sparking intuitive learning in the acquisition of scientific knowledge in mathematics, physics, chemistry, biology, physiology, and kinesiology.

As a unique way of achieving basketball excellence, *3fz* is also a scientific approach to exploring innate talents and resources of the human body, particularly of the hand and brain. For everyone is created equal with talents and potentials that exhibited in brilliant artists, scientists, and sport stars, *3fz* is an innovative way to explore these talents, especially for children.

The *3fz* cross-connect symmetric training stimulates intelligence between teaching and learning axes of the human body. From the training, youths will obtain balanced athletic systems, increased logic and intuitive intelligence, and comprehensive learning abilities. For basketball players, *3fz* training is a lifelong learning course of physiology and kinesiology, and they can apply physiodynamics and biomechanics into their physical body. The learning method, of taking theory directly into praxis, can be adapted to any theoretic learning to creative applications in vocations and life.

Challenges of Education

Education versus Sports

In elementary school, sports are a fun part of education; they bring pure benefits to children's physical and mental developments. Beginning in secondary school, it becomes more competitive, and some students exhibit talents for particular sport. They enjoy playing and training more for their favored sports, and many parents support their children to endeavor sport careers. They do substantial training and regular competitions in and out of school. From then on, their education and sports have diverged goals, and they encounter major conflicts in how they spend time and efforts on the different objectives.

Attracted by college sports scholarships and wealthy professional athletes, most talented young athletes take on sports career at early ages, with their caring parents' financial and physical support. Many students push so hard for early success in sports that they make school less of a priority. The school subjects become unimportant since colleges give scholarships to athletes with minimum grades of school subjects.

In universities, athletes put their utmost efforts into training and competition. The primary goal of college athletes and their academic institutions is to win competitions and bring glory to their schools. College education is their secondary objective. Each year, only a small group of elite college athletes could get into professional selections, such as NBA drafts, and the majority of them did not graduate.

Starting in high school, that is the track of a professional basketball player. However, most high school players are not so successful. Either they do not get college scholarships or they did get college scholarships but didn't make the NBA.

It is a serious problem in school education. High school students pursuing sports careers often have limited work on their school subjects such as sciences and literature. And college athletes spend a small portion of their time and effort in academic studies. Even if they earn a degree with their subpar course work, it is hard to make a career in the competitive marketplace after they graduate.

Career and Life Strategy

The objective of school education is to base a solid foundation for youths, with sufficient knowledge and physical wellness to build their careers and personal lives. School physical education has the goal of achieving full physical and mental development of children, and provides fundamental training in different sports. If they have a good education and a talent for sports, they can choose any kind of sports careers, such as athletes, researchers, or educators.

Contrary to the education objective, many young people choose the sports track in their early school years. Since so many children have physical and sports-specific talents in elementary school, only a handful of the best athletes are chosen each year by the major professional sports leagues. The chance of a talented athletic child entering a professional league such as the NBA is not much better than winning a lottery.

There are more reasons that youths should not get into the sports-career gambling. First, the competition sports are complex vocations with many scientific disciplines, and they won't be able to cope with the systems of training and competition without enough school education. Second, they need to be well educated to have meaningful lives outside of sports. Third, a sports career is a small part of an athlete's life; education is good for her entire life, long after sports.

Skills and Intelligence

Nowadays, sports skills and intelligence are contradictory in our modern society. The rare sports star has balanced talents and intelligence in sports and life. "Robust limbs, simple mind" seems a common symptom among athletes. It is also a fact among young people and college students that they are either good athletes and at the same time mediocre students, or vice versa.

Here is the problem with the current school sports. The skills that young people acquire in sport-specific training require limited knowledge and learning outside the game. Likewise, the knowledge of specific sports is not applicable in scientific subjects or academic studies. Players might have high basketball intelligence but low learning IQ of academic subjects. They could be great at basketball but lack the fundamental knowledge to pursue a vocation other than basketball.

In the beginning years, playing basketball, or even regular training, benefits the children in their physical and mental development. The game is a lot of fun, and they develop athletic skills, the spirit of teamwork, and communication skills. But after they have learned some solid fundamental skills, they start to think of getting more physically powerful like their idols, professional basketball players.

It is more convenient for them to pump up more muscles than to learn new stuff—and to play more basketball than to take on boring academic subjects. Their intelligence begins to decline at that stage. Many young basketball players lost their balance between sports and academics after they discovered that they had superior talents in certain sports.

3fz Education and Sports Solutions

Is there any sport that directly facilitates academic learning or becomes a part of it, not just as a physical and mental enhancement? There is no such sport, unless a child prodigy does a specific sport for scientific researches like young Mozart playing piano and composing. There is nearly always a problem with the balance of sports and education among young students.

The *3fz* conditioning and training, not just for basketball, has an innovative approach to solving this problem. It is an integration of education and sports for everyone.

- It is a two to three years or longer learning course, full of academic subjects, such as biology, physiology and kinesiology, and sports activities, in which every student will enjoy participating.
- The learning and practicing activities in this course will build solid sports skills with great development potential.
- The concepts and practices will spark intelligence of their left and right brains and enhance full physical and mental development.
- The knowledge and skills they acquire will help them understand their bodies and abilities for long-term educated self-training in sports, so that they do not need to gamble on having a sport career with just physical talents.

To implement this concept and approach to school education, basketball is the best sport to start with.

The *3fz* principles can also be applied to the physical education for children of elementary school. Although *3fz* is primarily a basketball skill, it is also a tool in achieving athletic and intellectual excellence. The *3fz* training will benefit children in their schools, careers, and future lives.

- The *3fz* explores their innate resources, especially in the hand and brain, for athletic talents and learning abilities. The *3fz* conditioning and *UniShot* training are innovative enhancements to physical, mental, and intelligent development of youths.
- Mastering *3fz* is an intensive learning process for children in the scientific principles of biology, physics, physiology, and mathematics. In *3fz* learning, they need to understand their bodies, biomechanics, and kinesiology in order to coach themselves with educated knowledge to achieve basketball excellence. They can adapt the creative learning methods to their studies of any level.
- In basketball, *3fz* eliminates the disadvantages of physical shortcomings in body heights and pure physical strengths. Players will gain more athletic abilities, ball-handling skills, and smart plays.
- Children need more intelligence and education to train for and play the game, since *3fz* gives equal opportunities for everyone in basketball. There will be no such shortcut as for the conventional basketball career with just having physical talents, since mastering *3fz* is an intelligent, long-term process of educated training.

In *3fz* and *UniShot* revolutionized basketball games, only the smartest, with assiduous work, can be the best.

Physical and Mental Development

From the age of six, children may start to play piano, as their fingers have developed enough strength. The keystrokes, the fingers and hand movements, harmonized with music, stimulate brain activity through the central nervous systems. Physiologically, each finger has the same amounts of neurons connecting through limbs to the brain. The hand has significantly more tactile (sensory) and motor cortices than other human body parts such as limbs, feet, or head.

Because it has the same low physical requirements as playing piano, children may start *3fz* training in elementary school. The basketball is big and round, and its surface is soft. It is great fun for children, as they can do many *3fz* tricks with it.

The *3fz* mechanism actively touches the ball with the fingertips, pads, and the MP palm. Its dynamic ball handling includes all coordinated movements of hand, fingers, and wrist, also involving coordination of other body parts: eyes, neck, arms, hips, ankles, knees, trunk, and feet. Practicing *3fz* will help develop children's physical and mental strengths: bone and muscle growth, agility, acuity, hand-eye coordination, endurance, and stamina.

Playing Sports

The *3fz* mechanism is primarily a basketball skill. It can be used as a tool of physical exercises or conditioning for other sports. The only requirements of *3fz* training are a basketball and a small confined space with a wall. It is better and more fun, but not necessary, to have a basket. Solo practice is the most enjoyable with *3fz* conditioning.

The *3fz* training involves most joints and muscle groups, and coordinates them to the fundamental moves of other sports: running, jumping, throwing, body turning, spinning, and twisting. The *3fz* symmetric training develops ambidexterity that can be adapted to any sport.

Mind and Body Integration

The *3fz* principles emphasize court vision and decision making while handling the ball. The method allows players to handle the basketball in protected fashions and have time and vision to make playing decisions. There are more thinking processes than subconscious plays.

The *3fz* training is a learning process, from dominant axis to weak axis. Its drills work different muscles, ligaments, and joints, building self-consciousness of their functions and involvements. The motor cortex transfers signals of muscle moves and coordination to the encephalon of the brain. The more active brain actions will be triggered by muscle and mind integration in different moves and shots.

Intellectual Exploration

Cross-connect symmetric training stimulates the learning activities between the contralateral axes of the body. In turn, the activities reflect to the left and right brains for logic and intuitive thinking. These complex learning systems explore the natural talents residing in the body and brain. The talents include sciences, arts, and sports, and they can be extremely useful in professional development.

Education and Vocation

Learning *3fz* involves the knowledge of math, physics, biology, physiology, anatomy, chemistry, and language. Children will practice *3fz* and *UniShot* basketball skills with educated training by knowing what, why, and how they do it. Learning by doing is the best way to improve in both theories and praxes. This way, with hands-on performing, the students can develop good learning habits. Then they will have enough theoretic knowledge of academic studies, which they can then apply into vocational praxes.

FUTURE GAME

A Perfect Game

The *3fz* revolution will advance basketball to a perfect game. The revolution will liberate basketball participants from the existing physical hazards and mental ugliness. The future game will produce great athletes, intellectual players, and healthy multi-aged basketball populations.

The game of every child's dream is shared by women, elders, and everyone—including Baron de Coubertin. It is water from the highest, washing the dirt away and revealing its original beauty and love. It replenishes us and offers joy, health, and longevity.

Playing New Games

The *3fz* basketball revolution brings fundamental changes in the ways we handle the basketball and how we play the game offensively and defensively. The *3fz* mechanism with its *4u1* establishes groundbreaking unification of fundamental basketball skills. *UniShot* driven by *3fz* will dominate the game with its superb shooting range and accuracy.

In the next ten years, the majority of players should be using *3fz* mechanism as their prime basketball skill in competitions. You will see more and more seniors, women, and educated or self-trained *UniShooters* in professional games. They will have more agility, coordination, endurance, and skills, with relatively smaller sizes and much lighter body weights. The game flow will be much faster, and offense executions more efficient, with elevated passing skills and teamwork.

UniShot yields high-shooting accuracies in long ranges; eventually the three-point arc will be extended and the basketball court rearranged. The defense will be more aggressive, with constant double-team in the perimeters. Players' athletics and *3fz* skills are keys of winning games.

Ambidextrous Long Shots

For releasing positions, the future shootings are three-dimensional: up-handed and underhanded, side shots and scissors shots, and low releases and high shots. There will be more ambidextrous, spectacular, and accurate shots such as high-spring, one-hand-only underhanded and up-handed shots; ear and head hook shots; swirl and twist shots; and so on. These shots can be accurately launched in three-point ranges, as the distance is relatively short to *UniShot*s.

Placing and Positioning

The future shootings will make full use of the offensive half court. When the clock is running down, high-percentage shots can launched anywhere in the half court to beat the buzzer. *UniShot*, the future shooting mechanism gives players good balanced abilities for high-arc shooting. Shots can be launched along the sidelines or behind the backboard, beyond the baseline. The existing three-point arc is relatively too close to the basket for the players with great leaping abilities, since they can jump far to launch fly-in three-pointers like a regular layup.

Offense Teamwork

The offense will be more dynamic since there are more accurate long shots and passes. High screens will be set more frequently to free space for *UniShooters*. The pace of offense will be much faster, with running, passing, and dynamic shooting. The offensive team will outrebound the defensive team since they have speed, open spaces, and good timing facing the basket. Long shots, fast breaks, and offensive rebounds will dominate the game.

Defense

Defensive teams will have a hard time in future games. They have to double-team *UniShooters* in the perimeters. There is no other choice because accurate *UniShot*s will dominate one-man coverage. Team defenses are hard to execute and physically demanding as well. Five players are not enough to defend a team with a *UniShooter*, because outside double-team leaves one offensive player open inside.

New Scoring Concept

The verb *shoot* is related to gun, bullet, and target. Shooting a basketball with the conventional method, your hands act as a gun, the ball as a bullet, and the basket as a target. With its quick shooting time and short pushing distance, it is a hard, explosive process. In the shooting process, you need to set the shot, aim at the basket, and shoot the ball out at the target with explosive power generated by your body, just like the gun shooting a bullet at a target.

The future scoring method is *propelling the ball into the basket,* not shooting it. In the process, your feet, legs, back, shoulder, arm, and hand coordinate as a well-designed launching machine. Your fingers control the ball in long pushing distance with accurate guides. In natural propelling mechanism, players can throw the ball freely into the basket; the basket is right under a well-projected trajectory in their guiding arm and hand. The throwing is a natural process of catching, lifting, swinging, and pushing with the dynamic powers generated by the whole body in accurate alignment. The ball is propelled into the basket in a long, smooth, and well-controlled natural pushing process with precise guiding.

Keys of the Propelling Process

- Maintain static or dynamic triple threat before launching.
- Keep good court vision and peripheral view of the target.
- Detect the defense and protect the whole propelling process.
- Feel the basket instead of looking at it, and keep balanced body.
- Coordinate whole body and propelling alignment with spring power.
- Control the three-stage propelling process by stopping anytime.
- Launch only clean throws.
- Follow each throw for possible rebound.

Future Basketball Court and Rules

The *3fz* and *UniShot* will revolutionize basketball offense and defense. The rules, the team settings, and even the dimensions of the existing basketball court are no longer suitable for the new games. With the same basketball facilities we have now, the game regulations and concepts should be fundamentally reconstructed.

In the existing game settings, there are many problems in *3fz* revolution:

- The three-point arc is too small since *UniShooters* can easily make three-pointers. Two-point shots will be worthless to attempt; even if you make it, you lose ball possession, and the other team will make a three-pointer in return.

- The court sizes are too small, since the players will move dynamically and cover more floors. There will be accurate long passes in transition; players need more space to run and jump.

- The free throw distance is too short, since big players can extend their long arms close to the basket and throw a hard-to-miss low-hand *UniShot*.

- The three-second zone is too small, since *UniShot* moves give players more dynamics and quick shots in the paint.

- Five players are not enough to defend an offensive team with a *UniShooter*. They need to double-team the shooter with the ball constantly, and the three-point areas are too wide to cover.

Future Court Design and Rule Changes

To meet the challenges *3fz* brings to the existing basketball court, the best way to do it is to have a new design of the court and some basic rule changes. This new design should keep the existing basketball facilities intact. The following are the future basketball court design and some new game rules:

1. The sideline extends 3 feet (1 meter) on each side, so the width of the court is 56 feet (17 meters) instead of 50 feet (15.24 meters).
2. The three-point arc has a radian of 28 feet (8.6 meters) from the rim center, and the arc is cut off with a parallel sideline of 26 feet, 6 inches (8 meters) to the rim. If the shooting foot or feet step on the line and a basket is made, it counts as three points.
3. The free throw line moves back by 4 feet, to 19 feet (5.7 meters) from the rim.
4. The three-second (paint) area is enlarged to accordingly cover 50 percent more of the floor. There is no no-charge zone.
5. The baselines extend backward for one foot (0.3 meter), so the court length is 96 feet (29.25 meters) instead of 94 feet (28.65 meters).
6. The effective area of the basketball court is borderline inclusive like the tennis court, as is the three-point area, the paint, and the offensive half court.
7. The game is played with seven players on each team: three guards, two forwards, and two centers.
8. Hand check and triple-team in defense are not allowed.
9. Two top corners of the backboard are cut off so its total area is reduced by 20 percent.
10. Half court exit time is six seconds, shot clock at twenty, and inbound throw at four seconds.
11. No backcourt violations, no team defense and offense technical fouls.
12. Individual dribbling limitations: five dribbles crosscourt, four in the same half court and three dribbles in the paint.
13. Four referees for the game, one at each borderline. Taped review only for tied decisions.

Back to the Nature, the Game of 3fz Revolution

"The best given to man is like water, which benefits all things without vying, which flows in places that others disdain, where it is in harmony with the Way.

Live the nature; think the deep; give the love; speak the truth; govern the order; craft the ability; act the opportunity.

Man does not contend, and none contend against him."

—*Tao Te Ching* No. 8

Laozi taught us the natural Tao of doing everything as it is originated. It should be like water—fluent, beautiful, harmonious, truthful, and powerful.

The basketball game will return to its origin, which is the spring of youthfulness, esthetics, intelligence, and magnificence. As the Tao taught by Laozi is for life and sports, the *3fz* mechanism is the Tao of playing basketball. It will bring the sport to its original beauty and high glory, to a perfect game.

Basketball will truly be

> ➤ A wonderful sport utilizing maximum human physical resources and athletic talents
> ➤ A delightful competition of pure skills and athletic excellence for all, regardless of age, gender, or size
> ➤ One of the most enjoyable games, full of accurate ranging shots, spectacular moves, and fluent team plays
> ➤ A beautiful game of sportsmanship, human virtues, and physical esthetics
> ➤ An exciting activity that enhances physical and mental development of youths and improves public health and human relationships
> ➤ A clean game that is played fair and just, free of dirty plays, malicious physical contact, or any misconduct
> ➤ A health competition sport that protects players from passive injuries and prevents cumulative injures so that they will have long sports lives
> ➤ Friendly competitions to win hearts and to bring love and peace.